THE LOVE FEAST

Compiled by Frank Ramirez

Brethren Press

The Love Feast
Compiled by Frank Ramirez

Unless otherwise noted, scripture text is from the New Revised Standard Version ®,
copyright © 1989, Division of Christian Education of the National Council of the
Churches of Christ in the United States of America.

"The Divine Servant" is the creation of Max Greiner, Jr. Used by permission. For
information on Greiner drawings, paintings, and sculpture, contact the artist at Max
Greiner, Jr. Designs ©, P.O. Box 290522, Kerrville, TX 78029-0522, (830) 896-7919.

Designed by Gwen M. Stamm

09 08 07 06 05 04 03 02 01 00   10 9 8 7 6 5 4 3 2 1

Library of Congress Cataloging in Publication Data
The love feast / compiled by Frank Ramirez.
        p. cm.
     Includes bibliographical references.
     ISBN (paperback): 0-87178-020-8
     ISBN (cloth): 0-87178-024-0
     1. Love feasts. 2. Foot washing (Rite). 3. Lord's Supper—Church of the Brethren.
  4. Church of the Brethren—Liturgy. I. Ramirez, Frank, 1954-

BX7825.5.L67 L68 2000
264'.065099—dc21   00-021478

Manufactured in the United States of America

To Frank and Delores Ramirez

who gave me my first and best religious instruction

through their word and example.

CONTENTS

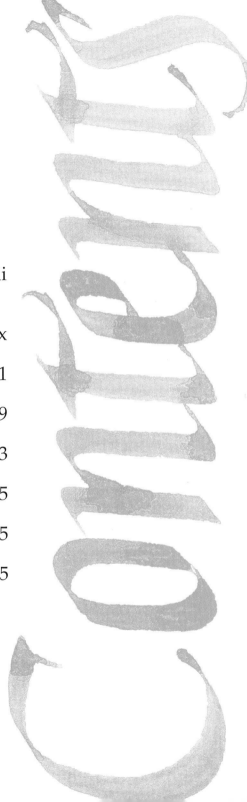

The ancient agape meal. Graydon Snyder Collection.

FOREWORD

BRETHREN pastor Frank Ramirez has compiled this treasury of love feast stories, history, worship resources, photos, art, music, and instructions with true affection. His love of the ordinance is all the more compelling because Frank is a "convinced" Brethren and not a birthright Brethren. He chose this group of faithful, imperfect feet and all, over, or maybe in addition to, his Catholic upbringing. Who more appropriate than he to reflect on this meaningful communitarian ritual.

Ramirez does more than reflect, however. He brings us important material from the ancients who first practiced the love feast and to whom Brethren looked for models. He follows the development of the love feast in Brethren history, including early standards and later diversions. He also provides us with practical helps for holding the love feast, such as recipes, orders of worship, music, and ways to adapt the ordinance for people with handicaps. He has dug up testimonies on the love feast and delved into some of the controversies surrounding it, such as whether communion could be served in a pew during worship without the other parts of the love feast, or how children and non-members could or could not participate. In all, Ramirez' collection speaks volumes about the Brethren.

It is possible to be too nostalgic about the love feast, romanticizing unity, servanthood, and the agape feast. By telling both the good and bad about love feast, Frank avoids such oversimplification. And by telling the occasional story of discord and failings of the Brethren, he rightly depicts the Brethren as a community that has been strengthened by tensions and refinements. Overall, the reader comes away, not with nostalgia, but with a greater understanding of a ritual that lives and continues to have meaning.

When Brethren were more sectarian, participation in love feast was closed to anyone but members, though observers commonly watched from a distance, sometimes in awe, sometimes deriding the odd ritual. While love feast is still for members, in many congregations the concept of membership is broad enough to include the occasional observer in the feast. In any case, all are invited to the feast in this book, participating in the mystery and the action through its stories and prayers. As principal founder of the Brethren Alexander Mack would likely have said, all will be welcome eventually to the Lord's table.

Julie Garber
Elgin, Illinois, 2000

PREFACE

THE FIRST BRETHREN took up the practice of the love feast out of nearly zealous adherence to scriptural teaching. They were spurred on not by some new revelation about how to live the Christian life, but by trying to recover the original intent of the early church, presuming that the earliest expression of Christian faith was closest to Jesus' intent. To recover the original church, layers and centuries of church traditions had to be peeled away and the old practices recovered by study and speculation.

The circumstances of their era in Europe left the early Brethren searching for a better way. By the late seventeenth century, Europe was completely torn apart by horrific wars, which princes and priests and pastors alike justified by a demonic twisting of Christianity. At the end of the war, the people of the Germanys lived under the Treaty of Westphalia, which required that the population of a province confess the same faith as its prince. Against a backdrop of growing religious cynicism, various alternative groups, such as the Anabaptists and the Pietists, demanded a return to the New Testament faith. At great cost to themselves in terms of torment and death, they managed to recreate what was to them God's true church reborn.

Some believers, in an attempt to more perfectly follow the word of God, came to believe that certain basic outward signs for Christ's church were called for in scripture. Primary among these was believer baptism, which was outlawed. Despite great personal risk, eight men and women, led by Alexander Mack, Sr., baptized each other in the Eder River near Schwarzenau, Germany, sometime in the summer of 1708. Because they intended to be Christ's church, neither named nor built upon any human name, they did not record the name of the person who baptized the first

minister, nor the day or exact place of these baptisms.

Within thirty years, and after much suffering and persecution, most Brethren had moved to the colonies in the New World to seek religious freedom. These people lived simple and honest lives, being in the world, yet not of the world. They took no name unto themselves, but called each other brethren, their word for the brothers and sisters. They followed Christ and took care of each other. Brethren spread across the country, endured persecution during times of war for their pacifist beliefs, and sought always to serve God and their neighbors.

Brethren practiced a simple lifestyle, remaining for many decades a people of the land. Together they sought to conform to the commands of scriptures and practice a biblical nonconformity with the aims of the world. Nevertheless, they did not retreat from their society, but sought to witness to it through the examples of their lives. They welcomed newcomers to their faith, practicing their own form of visitation evangelism.

Brethren have always sought God's will for their lives, at all times testing innovations against what seemed to them to be the leading of the Holy Spirit, including revival services, church schools, world missions, higher education, and church publications. Over time these brothers and sisters experienced painful schisms as they sought God's will for themselves in a changing world. But they also continued to grow, both in numbers and in faithfulness. They met the challenge of the emerging modern world by adapting to it externally but remaining, through joint study of scripture, as faithful as they could to the principles of the New Testament church.

Though the Brethren may have changed from one of the plain peoples over three hundred years, they have tried to remain faithful to their founding principles—that the blueprint for the church is to be found by Christians studying the scriptures together. We have not always succeeded, but we have been blessed in that God has chosen us, unworthy though we are, to carry out the command for the love feast and feetwashing, serving as a witness to word of the Lord.

Frank Ramirez
Elkhart, Indiana, 2000

We indeed have neither a new church or any new laws. We only want to remain in simplicity and true faith in the original church which Jesus founded through His blood. We wish to obey the commandment which was in the beginning.

—*Alexander Mack*

*I*T ALL BEGAN with the Prince of Peace. Before a fellowship meal at Passover to commemorate the liberating acts of God, the Lord of Life knelt before his followers and, taking on the aspect of a slave, performed the menial task of washing the disciples' feet, which he then commanded them to perform for each other.

Then the Brethren got involved. When the first Brethren met in Bible study in the early years of the eighteenth century, they studied scripture thoroughly to uncover and recreate the early church, stripping away centuries of traditions, interpretations, and corruptions. The furthest thing from the mind of the earliest Brethren was originality. It was not their intention to create a new thing, but to recover an old thing.

Brethren were almost zealous in their effort to do all that Jesus commands in scripture, including nonresistance, nonconformity, and avoidance of oath-taking. As Dale Stoffer notes in his essay in *The Lord's Supper*, "The Brethren, following the Mennonites, were committed to complete obedience to all Christ's commands and examples. In this, the early Brethren were quite scrupulous. They went beyond the Mennonites in insisting, for example, not only on adult baptism, but adult baptism by immersion; likewise, they went beyond Mennonites in maintaining that feetwashing and the love feast were ordinances that should be observed with communion."

In John's Gospel, Brethren found in one single story the instruction for all the components of what became known to them as the love feast: an actual meal, a form of the bread and cup communion familiar throughout Christendom, and a clear message to wash each other's feet following the example of their Lord. Only John brings together all the components of the rite that are scattered in the other Gospel accounts of the Passion and in the Epistles.

2

Whoever wishes to
become great among you
must be your servant, and
whoever wishes to be first
among you must be slave
of all. For the Son of Man
came not to be served but
to serve, and to give his
life a ransom for many.
—*Mark 10:43-45*

"The Divine Servant," ® *based on Mark 10:43-45, is the copyrighted and trademarked creation of artist, Max Greiner, Jr.*

This is why it happened that our brethren in Schwarzenau found in their diligent study in the witness of John that Christ our Lord, the last night before the supper, washed the feet of His disciples and also commanded that they too should wash one another's feet.

—*Sander Mack to Brother John Preisz on the Indian Creek,* The Brethren in Colonial America

Ancient origins of the love feast

In addition to the biblical mandate, Brethren drew the practice of the love feast from the early church. There are many mentions of both feetwashing and fellowship meals in the first centuries of the church, after which the Catholic mass evolved and veritably replaced the more elaborate practice of the love feast.

What did the practice look like in the ancient church? Brethren have felt all along—and more and more historians are beginning to agree—that one could find a recognizable love feast in the ancient church that resembles modern Brethren tradition, especially in the combination of feetwashing, the Lord's Supper, and the bread and cup.

The inaugural love feast with Jesus and the disciples immediately became an institution practiced among the apostles, according to this account in the *Apostolic Constitutions,* the recorded writings of the original disciples.

> We ought therefore also to serve the brethren, in imitation of Christ, for says He, "He that will be great among you, let him be your minister, and he that will be first among you, let him be your servant." For so did He really, and not in word only, fulfill the prediction of, "serving many faithfully." For "when He had taken a towel, He girded Himself. Afterward He puts water into a basin; and as we were sitting at home, He came and washed the feet of us all, and wiped them with the towel." By doing this He demonstrated to us His Kindness and bore affection so that we also might do the same to one another. If, therefore, our Lord and Master so humbled himself, how can you, the laborers of the truth, and adminstrators of piety, be ashamed to do the same to such of the brethren as are weak and infirm?

The genius of the early Christian movement is that its membership cut across not only racial but also economic lines, the two chief ways of segregating the modern church. Then, both slaves and homeowners worshiped together. The earliest Christian communions probably resembled the typical modern church potluck, with individuals bringing food to share for the love feast, meeting in homes of members. The first-century church, as in our own

During supper Jesus, knowing that the Father had given all things into his hands, and that he had come from God and was going to God, got up from the table, took off his outer robe, and tied a towel around himself. Then he poured water into a basin and began to wash the disciples' feet and to wipe them with the towel that was tied around him.

—*John 13:3-5*

era, witnessed great disparities in personal income among members. Therefore, the communion table was a rare focal point for equality.

The earliest Christians were recalling in these communion services not only the last supper but the feeding of the five thousand, an event in which all ate and were satisfied. Representations of communion in early Christian art consistently include symbols of that particular miracle. For the poor of society, who rarely ate meat or even ate well, this sort of feasting was a clear foreshadowing of the kingdom as expressed both in the words of Jesus and in the pages of the Hebrew prophets.

It would be wrong, however, to think that the early church was able to overcome all barriers and prejudices. That the administration of communion did not always go smoothly is attested to in Paul's letter to the Corinthians, where he accuses the rich and leisured Christians of finishing the good food before the poor people arrive from their work (1 Cor. 11:17-22). But done well or poorly, the love feast was practiced from the beginning of Christendom.

Beyond the first century

The practice of the love feast continues past the first Christian century. The pagan administrator Pliny the Younger wrote to the emperor Trajan around A.D. 112 about the Christians who lived in his district. At that time there were rumors spreading about the Christian meal, suggesting it was cannibalistic because Christians were eating the "body" of Christ. Pliny reported, after questioning those who renounced Christianity, that when Christians gathered together in worship they ate only ordinary food. This is similar to the practice of Brethren today, where ordinary food is prepared in homespun fashion to be made a part of a holy meal.

That the full love feast was still practiced, complete with feetwashing and the agape meal in the second century after Christ, is clear from Tertullian's description in *The Apology* 39 written in A.D. 197.

> Our feast explains itself by its name. The Greeks call it *agape*, i.e., affection. Whatever it costs, our outlay in the name of piety is gain, since with the good things of the feast we benefit the needy; not as it

The ancient love feast was more like a potluck meal than communion, more like feeding the multitudes than eucharist. Loaves and fishes in ancient artwork depict the love feast and allude to the gospel stories of Jesus feeding a crowd of thousands. Graydon Snyder Collection.

PS: After ending this [letter] I have received a detailed report about the new Anabaptists in the Schwarzenau area. They also observe feet-washing and communion, but refuse to let anyone participate who has not been baptized by them with water. And because all new sectarianism produces zeal, this is also true with them. When, however, this fiery ardor has burned down, then the zeal will lessen of itself. April 20, 1709

—*John George Gichtel
(1638–1710) in* European Origins
of the Brethren

is with you, do parasites aspire to the glory of satisfying their licentious propensities, selling themselves for a belly feast to all disgraceful treatment, but as it is with God himself, a peculiar respect is shown to the lowly. If the object of our feast be good, in the light of that consider our further regulations. As it is an act of religious service, it permits no vileness or immodesty. The participants before reclining, taste first of prayer to God. As much is eaten as satisfies the craving of hunger, as much is drunk as befits the chaste. They say it is enough, as those who remember that even during the night they have to worship God; They talk as those who know that the Lord is one of their auditors. After manual ablution [feetwashing], and the bringing in of lights, each is asked to stand forth and sing, as he can, a hymn to God, either one from the Holy Scriptures, or one of his own composing—a proof of the measure of our drinking.

Origen, a Christian theologian and scholar from Alexandria, is also from the second century. He tells us not only that there were love feasts in the early years, but that opponents of Christianity scorned the practice.

> The first point Celsus brings forward, in his desire to throw discredit upon Christians, is that the Christians entered into secret societies . . . . And his wish is to bring into disrepute what are termed the "love-feasts" of the Christians. (*Ante-Nicene Fathers*, IV)

Then in the third century, Cyprian, Bishop of Carthage, lived and died a Christian martyr. He also talks about the love feast in his writings.

> Let them imitate the Lord, who at the very time of His passion was not more proud, but more humble. For then he washed His disciples' feet, saying, "If I, your Lord and Master, have washed your feet, ye ought also to wash one another's feet. For I have been given you an example, that he should do as I have done to you." (*Ante-Nicene Fathers*, V)

In the fourth century, Bishop Ambrose of Milan wrote in *Of the Holy Spirit* (1:14):

Somewhere near these farms above Schwarzenau, Germany, Alexander Mack and seven other believers met together and baptized one another as Brethren. In their search for authentic Christian practice, they reclaimed the full love feast of scripture and the early Christian church. BHLA Collection.

I, then, wish also myself to wash the feet of my brethren, I wish to fulfill the commandment of my Lord, I will not be ashamed in myself, nor disdain what He Himself did first.

Jerome (ca. 340–420) is well known for translating the Bible into vulgate, opening the world of scriptures to the masses. The demonstration of Christ's love for all, even the slave, in feetwashing fits well with his effort to bring the Bible to more than the learned church scholar and bureaucrat. Of feetwashing, he says:

> For example, Our Lord in the Gospel is girt with a towel, He prepares a basin to wash the disciples' feet, He performs the service of a slave. Granted, it is to teach humility, that we may minister to each other in turn. I do not deny that. I do not reject it. What is it that He says to Peter upon his refusal? If I wash not thy feet, thou shalt have no part with me. And he replied: Lord, not only my feet, but also my hands and my head. (*Nicene and Post-Nicene Fathers*)

By the time of St. John Chrysostom (ca. 347–ca. 407) in the late fourth century, the love feast had become a centuries-old tradition. Still, the practice of the feast he describes is not much different from the earliest accounts. In fact, his discussion of feetwashing raises the same questions Peter raised at the original feast: "Lord, are you going to wash my feet? . . . You will never wash my feet" (John 13:6-8).

> "Let us wash one another's feet," He said. "Those of slaves, too?" and what great thing is it, even if we do wash the feet of slaves? For He Himself was Lord by nature, while we were slaves, yet He did not beg off from doing even this . . .Yet what shall we then say, we who have received the example of such great forbearance, but do not imitate it even slightly, and who, on the contrary, adopt the opposite attitude: both magnifying ourselves unduly and not rendering to others what we ought? (*Commentary on Saint John the Apostle and Evangelist*, Homilies 48-88)

This sarcophagus from Arles is called **Aqua** *because Jesus washes the disciples feet at left and Pilate washes his hands at right. In the very center is Jesus at the final judgment. At his right and left are the apostles.* Graydon Snyder Collection.

By the fifth century, the Holy Roman Church defined the center of Christendom in Rome and brought the practice of the love feast, traditionally held in private homes or cemeteries, into the church in the form of the mass. Then the love feast as the full reenactment of feetwashing and the agape meal practically disappears from view until a very few groups, such as the Brethren, recover it in the eighteenth century.

Starting over

Nadine Pence Frantz, professor of theology at Bethany Theological Seminary, notes in *Anabaptist Currents* that "different traditions typify themselves as 'people of the Word.' What they mean by this is that they are Christians whose self-definition and self-identity reside in some sort of relationship with the fact that they read the Bible."

She goes on to say "the Believers' Church tradition . . . is a self-corrective to this orientation. . . . *doing* the Word is the heart of the matter.

" . . . the way [Brethren] 'do' the Lord's Supper . . . [has] as much to do with who they are and how they envision God's presence in the world as do times of action and service in the world" (153-155).

Alexander Mack, the prime mover behind the birth of the Brethren, lays out a way of "doing the word," which Don Durnbaugh summarizes by saying,

> (1) the Scriptures are the standard of authority; (2) the Scriptures are to be interpreted by the Holy Spirit, ruling out a strict biblicism; (3) the presence of the Spirit is tested within the covenanting community; (4) there is a binding quality to covenant; (5) brethren should forbear one another in love, at the same time expecting that unity of belief will be given to those who persist; (6) truth is dynamic, and long usage and tradition must be discarded when they hamper the search for truth. (*Brethren Life & Thought*, Summer 1967)

This final point is what caused the Brethren to search for the original love feast as it was before it was enshrined in church doctrine and tradition, and to retrieve it as a central ordinance of the faith community.

The Brethern's Card.

Be it known to all men:

That there is a people who, as little children (Luke 18:17), accept the Word of the New Testament as a message from Heaven (Heb. 1:1, 2), and teach it in full (2 Tim. 4:1, 2, Matt. 28:20.)

They baptize believers by trine immersion (Matt. 28:19), with a forward action (Rom. 6:5), and for the remission of sins (Acts 2:38), and lay hands on those baptized, asking upon them the gift of God's Spirit (Acts 19:5, 6).

They follow the command and example of washing one another's feet (John 13:4, 17).

They take the Lord's Supper at night (John 13:30), at one and the same time, tarrying one for another (1 Cor. 11:33, 34).

They greet one and another with a holy kiss (Acts 20:37; Rom. 16:16).

They take the communion at night, after supper, as did the Lord (Mark 14:17:23).

They teach all the doctrines of Christ, peace (Heb. 12:14), love (1 Cor. 13), unity (Eph. 4), both faith and works (James 2:17, 20).

They labor for nonconformity to the world in its vain and wicked custom (Rom. 12:2).

They advocate nonswearing (Matt. 5:34, 37), antisecretism (2 Cor. 6:14, 17), opposition to war (John 18:36), doing good unto all men (Matt. 5:44, 46).

They annoint and lay hands on the sick (James 5:14, 15).

They give the Bread of Life, the message of the common salvation unto all men without money or price (Matt. 10:8).

Dear reader for the above we contend earnestly, and you, with all men, are entreated to hear, to examine and accept it as the word, which began to be spoken by the Lord, and the faith once delivered to the saints (Jude 3).

The above principals are briefly explained in tract form and will be sent with a catalogue of the publications of the Committtee free, to anyone by addressing the General Mission Board, Elgin, Illinois.

Our Sacred Promises.

———

I. Do you believe that Jesus Christ was the Son of God and that he brought a saving gospel from Heaven?

II. Do you willingly renounce Satan in all his pernicious ways and all the sinfull pleasures of the world?

III- Do you promise before God to live faithful until death?

≡

Suggestions

———

I. Read your Bible daily.—Acts 17:11.

II. Be sure and offer a short prayer each day.—Luke 11:1.

III. Be sure and choose good associates,—1 Cor. 15:33.

V. Be a worker.—Ecc. 9:10.

Yours in Christ's stead,

J. H. FIKE,

Middlebury, Ind.

Though put off by doctrinal statements, Brethren have at times tried to distill Brethren beliefs into brief statements. The Brethern's [sic] Card *lists feetwashing and love feast second after baptism in the short list of beliefs. BHLA Collection.*

When supper is prepared it is a mistake, or at least a want of fitness, for a brother to offer the verse: "Be present at our table, Lord." We having surrounded the Lord's table, it is therefore at *His* table, and *not our* table, that we desire the Lord's presence, hence our sentiment should be; "Be present at Thy table, Lord."

—*I. J. Rosenberger,* The Gospel Messenger, *July 24, 1883*

Early Brethren love feasts

For many years Brethren love feasts were affairs lasting two to three days and included not only members of the local fellowship, but Brethren from far and wide. Host congregations would provide housing and food for all the guests. Barns were cleared so all could sleep in comfort. Delicacies were prepared for the meals before and after love feast. And those not of the faith would sometimes gather outside just to watch, and sometimes deride, the proceedings.

As they studied their Bibles and church history, the Brethren found biblical and historical warrant for the four-fold communion (preparation, feetwashing, Lord's Supper, bread and cup) they practice today. In John's Gospel they read that Jesus told the disciples to follow his example and wash each other's feet. Then the apostles sat down with Jesus to a real meal. And they shared the bread and the cup. Brethren figured they had better do the same.

Over the centuries Brethren have been tinkering with the service to get things right. As a way of preparing physically and spiritually, Brethren added the deacon visit in which deacons would go in pairs to visit the brothers and sisters to see if all was right with the congregation. Now a self-examination service immediately before the ritual takes the place of this visit.

Brethren used to use wine. Now grape juice is the beverage of choice rather than wine. Brethren have at various times practiced either the "double mode" or the "single mode" of feetwashing, finally settling on the single mode. There was also a time when sisters did not break the bread with each other, but had it broken for them.

At one time nonmembers, mostly children, were not allowed to take part in the love feast except as observers. Now congregations allow varying degrees of partipation by nonmembers. Love feast has been open to outsiders, then closed, and is now again open. Bread has been prepared in several "official" ways over the years. The love feast used to take three days. Now it usually takes less than three hours. Ironically, with all the labor-saving devices of the modern era, people have less time than ever. Who can imagine setting aside three days of their lives for a church event and expect that everyone else in the church will set aside the same three days?

So Brethren have proceeded slowly and carefully, keeping in mind that

D. D. Funderburg, Maynard Cassady, and H. Spenser Minnich wash their feet in the Eder River on a 1925 pilgrimage to the site of the first Brethren baptisms. BHLA Collection.

we want to walk where Jesus walked—joyfully and with anticipation. On the one hand, it might have been nice to have a camera at the church's first love feasts, both in the ancient world and in the new world. On the other hand, photographs, like words, only tell part of the story, for the lens cannot capture what happens within the individual, something strong and eternal. Does the Brethren love feast look like the early Christian love feast? Yes and no. Is the intent the same? to follow Jesus? to do as he commanded? Without question.

The Brethren experiment is based upon a simple premise. We want to do what Jesus told us to do. It's easy for that simple statement to sound arrogant. But doesn't every Christian strive to do what Jesus told us to do? Doesn't every Christian search the New Testament for clues to how they can walk in Jesus' footsteps?

Many biblical literalists insist on taking one particular command of Jesus symbolically, that is, to wash one another's feet. In this they are no different from the scholars and advocates of higher biblical criticism. Almost no commentaries on John seem interested in whether the early church practiced feetwashing in obedience to Jesus. So perhaps the Brethren have been slow in thinking our way around John 13 and the rest of the communion scriptures. Jesus says we should wash feet. We wash feet. The text says we should share a meal. So we eat something. Even though many Brethren have adopted simple bread and cup communion on occasion and even though our own attendance has dropped, we have preserved this treasure of feetwashing, almost against our will, for the rest of the world. *F.R.*

The early agape meal was a fellowship meal that was often celebrated as a meal for the dead, or a refrigerarium. *Eventually, refrigeraria became meals for the martyrs. The* fractio panis *or breaking of bread depicted here is a refrigerarium celebrating the life of a Christian. Graydon Snyder Collection.*

There were two forms of communion: the *anamnesis*, or the remembering of the death and resurrection of Jesus, and the fellowship meal, which was an eschatological meal of the faith community. The fellowship meal was an *agape*, a love feast.

The agape meal served as both a welfare meal and a community-forming meal, but probably slid into the Greco-Roman meal for the dead, which is a meal celebrated on the anniversary of the death of a loved one, or more often. The meal with the dead wasn't superstitious. In those days people believed in a family that extended beyond the grave. As extended families they ate together at least once a year. Later, we see that many of these *refrigeraria* shifted to meals with the martyrs.

I argue that after Constantine the meals for the dead got out of hand, and finally Augustine and other friends decided they had to get control of them. They stopped the meals for the dead outside the city and brought them into the city and put the remembrance for the martyrs in the central part of the liturgy, at the altar. From here the agape runs into the mass.

Until the fourth century, in all pictures of the Agape, there were seven baskets and almost always seven people and almost always two fish. That symbolism I find impossible to deny. That's the heavenly banquet.

If [after 300 years] the Brethren need renewal, a recovery of the essential church, I would say it needs to stand off from the culture. It needs to come together in potlucks. It needs to come together as the community monthly or weekly without worry of liturgical and legal rules, but allowing the church to be the community. If you can move the love feast into the service of love rather than make it a formal thing, you may have your finger on church renewal.

—*Graydon F. Snyder, Chicago, Illinois*

PREPARATION

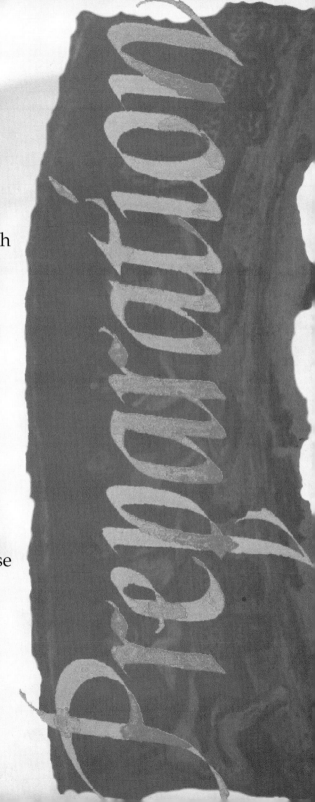

Bro John Eshelman reports his visit on north side of district. They found a serious trouble between Bro Kaufman and Bro Cozier.

Bro Kaufman accuses Cozier for taking more than his share of oats. Cozier sold a load of oats and did not account for it. Cozier is not present. A special Council is appointed for his case next Tuesday 1 week at 9 o'clock a.m. to be held at Arnold's Grove. After Council the Meeting house is to be put in order for the Love-Feast.

—*Arnold's Grove, Council Meeting minutes,*
   September 1, 1888

ITS VERY NAME, the love feast, suggests that it is a celebration of unity and fellowship in the body of Christ. Those who attend lay aside hard feelings, amend their ways, and settle conflicts with other members before approaching a common table, at least in theory. Even in Paul's time, however, the church abused the love feast by gathering without unity and without love. Neither is the church today, being a collection of human beings, always perfectly unified when it comes together, though that is what it strives for.

In his longest writing, *Rights and Ordinances*, Alexander Mack delineates the beliefs of the church in a clever conversation between father and son. At one point, the son asks, "Can obvious sinners be permitted at the Lord's Supper?" The father answers, "Obvious sinners cannot be permitted at the Lord's Supper, even if but one work of the flesh is evident in them [about which Paul writes in Galatians 5], if repentance or improvement does not take place after admonishment."

To this end the Brethren have set aside time before the love feast to prepare spiritually and relationally. In addition to preparing huge quantities of food and making dozens of places for visiting members to sleep in homes and barns and the attics of meetinghouses, deacons in each congregation would visit all members in their care before the love feast to ask about members' readiness to commune at the Lord's table. If deacons became aware of personal transgressions or interpersonal conflicts, they would report the problem to a congregational council meeting shortly before love feast. The council would consider each case, deliver admonishments or a course of discipline, and either invite the offenders to come to love feast (if an admonishment sufficed) or order them to "sit back from the table" as part of church discipline.

In the days when congregations encompassed wide geographic areas, members traveled some distance to love feast, needing overnight accommodations, often for several nights. Beds and mattresses were made up in the attics of churches, as pictured here, or in homes and barns of nearby members. Those who came to love feast more than a day early helped with all the preparations involved in hosting groups as large as several hundred members and observers. BHLA Collection.

Congregations practiced the deacon visit and church discipline in various ways and to varying degrees. No written guidelines existed until Annual Meeting minutes of 1867, which institutionalized the visit. Then in 1887, H. B. Brumbaugh wrote the first church manual, called *The Brethren's Church Manual*, that regularized practices such as the deacon visit.

For the church visit there is no direct scriptural authority, but it has always been a practice of the church as a means to an end. The end desired is that all the members may be in unity and peace, so that they may participate in the Communion services in a worthy manner (I Cor 11:27).

The visit is made by the deacons of the church, it being part of their official duty. . . . The design of the visit is to determine the spiritual condition of the members, and if there is any trouble existing in the minds of any in regard to their faith, or any trouble between member and member, it is the duty of those making the visit to inquire into the nature of such troubles and, as far as possible, assist in having them satisfactorily adjusted and removed. If this cannot be done, they must be reported to the church.

The visit is made prior to the Communion meetings, and it is thought best that two should go together and go from house to house. The importance of this visit cannot be overestimated, and therefore it should be made with great care, taking time enough at each house, when practicable, to have a season of worship with the family. . . .

After all the members have been visited, the deacons, or those who made the visit, report what they have found, or the condition of the members, at a church-meeting appointed for the purpose and to make the necessary arrangements for the communion service.
—*The Brethren's Church Manual*, H. B. Brumbaugh, 1887

The annual visit could be a time to catch up on all the large and small doings of a family and to find out if they had needs the congregation should be made aware of. Individuals' concerns about church matters could end up on the agenda of church council meetings. These in turn might eventually

An Invitation to Love Feast

Jesus Christ
Our beloved Savior and Lord
requests your presence at
a love feast
to be held in his honor
at seven o'clock
in the evening
—*James Benedict,
Union Bridge, Maryland*

THE BRETHREN'S CHURCH MANUAL,

CONTAINING

THE DECLARATION OF FAITH, RULES OF ORDER, HOW TO CONDUCT RELIGIOUS MEETINGS, &c.

BY

H. B. BRUMBAUGH.

"Let all things be done decently and in order."
1 Cor. xiv. 40.

BRETHREN'S PUBLISHING COMPANY,
HUNTINGDON, PA., & MT. MORRIS, ILL.
1887.

The first manual for congregations regularized for the first time practices such as the deacon visit, Sunday school, and parliamentary procedure, but not love feast. At the time, Brethren were still not of one mind on the mode of feetwashing.
BHLA Collection.

---

cases of necessity, lay members may also be called upon to assist in the visit.

The design of the visit is to determine the spiritual condition of the members, and if there is any trouble existing in the minds of any in regard to their faith, or any trouble between member and member, it is the duty of those making the visit to inquire into the nature of such troubles, and as far as possible assist in having them satisfactorily adjusted and removed. If this cannot be done, they must be reported to the church.

The visit is made prior to the Communion meetings, and it is thought best that two should go together and go from house to house. The importance of this visit cannot be overestimated, and therefore it should be made with great care, taking time enough at each house, when practicable, to have a season of worship with the family.

As a guide to the character of the visit the following form of questions has been submitted:

1. Are you still in the faith of the Gospel, as you declared when you were baptized?
2. Are you, as far as you know, in peace and union with the Church?

3. Will you still labor with the Brethren for an increase of holiness, both in yourself and others?

4. Liberty should be given to members to bring anything they may desire to, and they may think the good of the Church requires, before the visiting brethren.

After all the members have been visited, the deacons, or those who make the visit, report what they have found, or the condition of the members, at a church meeting appointed for the purpose and to make the necessary arrangements for Communion services.

CHAPTER XI.

CHURCH OFFICERS.

Bishop, or Elder.—The Elder, in addition to his ministerial duties, has the general oversight of the church in which he resides; he is to call council meetings when necessary, outside of the regular monthly or quarterly meetings; to act as Moderator in church and business meetings; to administer the ordinances of the Gospel, or to see that it is done by the other ministers, and to anoint the sick when called to do so. The elder receives his official position by request of the church in which he resides, and by approval of

Litany of Preparation

ONE: Bless the Lord, O my soul; and all that is within me,
   bless his holy name.

 ALL: Bless the Lord, O my soul, and forget not his benefits.

ONE: God forgives all our iniquities. God heals all our
   diseases.

 ALL: God redeems our lives from destruction; he crowns
   us with loving kindness and tender mercies.

ONE: The Lord is merciful and gracious, slow to anger,
   and plenteous in mercy.

 ALL: Bless the Lord, O my soul!

—*Valentina Satvedi, Vista, California*

end up at Annual Meeting, so that the questions addressed by the entire denomination had their foundation in the local membership of the church. This is precisely how a lone woman from Iowa named Julia Gilbert brought her objections to Annual Meeting regarding the prohibition against women serving communion to each other.

In the twentieth century, some of the duties vested in the deacons were taken over by ministers as they moved from free ministry to paid ministry. These paid ministers felt as if the care of the congregation fell to them and, in some cases, resented the power exerted by deacons. Evidence of this friction can be seen in this sentence from Brumbaugh's *Church Manual*:

> Ministers have the liberty to make, or assist in making, the visit if they think it best that they should do so, especially in cases where deacons have had no experience in this kind of church work. In cases of necessity, lay-members may also be called upon to assist in the visit.

With the rise of the professional pastorate, clearly some began to question the competency of so-called untrained deacons. By 1947 the annual visit was no longer listed as an official duty of the office of deacon.

The deacon visit, still practiced among some of the Old Order German Baptist Brethren, is rarely practiced today among Church of the Brethren congregations. It has been replaced by the examination service that precedes most celebrations of the love feast. Some people say that the deacon visit was a good idea and it's too bad we don't practice it anymore, but they often acknowledge that there isn't time to do it. It's curious, however, that with our cars and phones, we can't touch base with everyone in the congregation when our forebears managed to do it on horseback and foot!

More recently, congregations have returned to appointing deacons. And there is a feeling in some corners that a renewed deacon body should reinstitute the annual visit, perhaps as part of an undershepherd program. In *Called to Caregiving*, the manual for deacons, Karen Peterson Miller argues that there is a great call for caregiving in congregations, beyond what a pastor can do singlehandedly.

201 Just As I Am, Without One Plea

CHARLOTTE ELLIOTT, 1836   WOODWORTH   WILLIAM B. BRADBURY, 1849

1. Just as I am, with-out one plea, But that Thy blood was shed for me,
2. Just as I am, and wait-ing not To rid my soul of one dark blot,
3. Just as I am, tho' tossed a-bout With many a con-flict, many a doubt,
4. Just as I am, poor, wretched, blind; Sight, rich-es, heal-ing of the mind,
5. Just as I am! Thou wilt re-ceive, Wilt wel-come, par-don, cleanse, re-lieve;

And that Thou bidd'st me come to Thee, O Lamb of God, I come, I come.
To Thee whose blood can cleanse each spot, O Lamb of God, I come, I come.
Fight-ings and fears with-in, with-out, O Lamb of God, I come, I come.
Yea, all I need, in Thee to find, O Lamb of God, I come, I come.
Be-cause Thy prom-ise I be-lieve, O Lamb of God, I come, I come.

"Just as I am" is a common confessional hymn used in the service of preparation for love feast. Brethren prepare for love feast by confessing individual failings and repairing broken relationships with other members to unify the congregation. This version of "Just as I am" appeared in Hymnal *(1925) rendered in shaped notes, a system for reading music without accompaniment.*

O God, my prayer is simple. Show me to myself. Open my eyes that I may see myself as you see me. Strip away all sins that blind me, aid my memory and awaken my conscience. Help me to see what I have done to offend your love for me. Forgive me of all my sins; I need your mercy and grace. Help me now to experience your presence, healing, and strengthening touch throughout our love feast experience. This we seek through our Savior, Jesus Christ, Amen.

—*Jeff Glass, San Diego, California*

O gracious Host, whose guests have come
From south and north, from west and east,
Your welcome draws us to one home,
By invitation to one feast.

Apart we live, yet hearts are knit
In fellowship as hand meets hand.
Around one table we may sit,
One church, one company, one band.

Let none be lonely, bound, or broken;
Let none be alien to another.
We know the living Word has spoken
To claim each sister and each brother.

Though many separate ways we take,
Scattered to east, west, south, and north,
One cup we drink, one bread we break,
One table circles all the earth.

—Kenneth I. Morse, "A Hymn for World Communion" (1963)

Revitalizing the deacons' visit, where people minister to and with each other, can be a significant way of responding to that call. Perhaps the questions asked in the visit could be reformulated using the following wording:

1. Are you growing in the Christian faith?
2. As far as you are able to discern, are you at peace with your sisters and brothers?
3. How might you become a better steward of your talents and resources so that Christ may live more fully in you and others?
4. How might the congregation be more helpful to you in becoming a better steward of your spiritual gifts?

In some ways, preparation for love feast has changed dramatically since Alexander Mack's strident insistence on finding and excluding sinners. Most Brethren do not forbid outsiders today. It finally became counterproductive to turn away fascinated observers, not to mention the awkwardness of feasting in front of people with no food. Something holy was about to happen and the spectators could not participate in it. Some churches still refuse to admit nonmembers to love feast. Others believe that all are called to the Lord's table, noting that at the original Last Supper even Judas Iscariot was present.

Public confession of sin and church admonitions have turned into private examination and self-discipline. The strict ban against sinners at love feast has been relaxed to recognize that all have sinned and fallen short of the glory of God. Even the questions the deacons used to ask members are now reworded for private consideration. But interest in the unity of the body has not waned, even though the body has broadened considerably and unity is perhaps more difficult. Love feast is still one of the main things that keeps the body together. *F.R.*

Pews that made into tables for love feast were an ingenious invention of the Brethren. Before meetinghouses had fellowship halls, the sanctuary was the only place to conduct the love feast. Pews were hinged, allowing the back to roll up to form a table top or roll completely over, making a bench that faced the opposite direction. Pews pictured here are housed in the Germantown (Pennsylvania) meetinghouse, the mother church of the Brethren in America. BHLA Collection.

Hand-hewn bench used in the Heidelberg meetinghouse in Reistville, Pennsylvania.
Photo by E. G. Hoff (BHLA Collection).

There was a knock at my door. I thought perhaps the women's group needed help setting up tables and chairs, or maybe there was a question about the order of service, or—more likely—someone just wanted to stick their head in and say hi. "Come in," I said. And thus began one of the most interesting ministry encounters I have had in nearly fifteen years of full-time ministry.

It was an older gentleman I didn't recognize. He was wearing a wrinkled suit and an old-fashioned narrow tie. He had a thick shock of white hair, a big smile, and a suitcase in each hand. He also had a story to tell. It was a long story, which came out in bits and pieces, some of them repeated a couple of times.

One hundred and fifty years ago this man's great grandfather was an elder in a neighboring Brethren congregation. The elder's daughter, my visitor's grandmother, was raised in the church and eventually married a young man who was also Brethren. For a time, the younger couple was faithful and active in the life of the church. But then the elder's son-in-law got the notion to go to a county fair—an activity frowned upon as "worldly" by the congregation.

When word got out that the young man had attended the fair, he and his wife were visited by deacons and the man was admonished. Angered by the confrontation and headstrong (according to his grandson), the young man decided to leave the church rather than seek reconciliation. Torn between faithfulness to her church and to her spouse, the elder's daughter soon followed her husband out of the church.

Years later, when my visitor was just a young boy, his father (son of the fair-going man) died in the flu epidemic and the boy was sent to live with these grandparents who by this time had been separated from the Brethren for more than a quarter century. But the boy's grandmother still held the Brethren faith in high regard. In many ways it remained her faith; none other could replace it. She taught her grandson about Brethren beliefs and practiced as much of the faith as she could apart from a congregation. She also passed along her regret about the break with the congregation and the pain it still caused her.

My visitor explained that this time with his grandmother had been mostly forgotten as he had gone on to college, spent forty years as a pilot for a major airline, and raised two daughters of his own. But in the last few years, he found himself thinking about it often. It felt like a wound that was crying out for healing. Finally, at age eighty-seven, he decided to try to do something about it. Because he was legally blind, he asked his wife to drive him to the bus station. There he purchased the tickets and transfers for an eight-hundred-mile journey. With layovers the trip had taken twenty-three hours. Then there was a forty-five-minute taxi ride from a nearby city to my small town church.

After hearing the man's story, I was able to find an older deacon couple who had an idea where this man's grandmother had lived as a girl. We took a drive to that farm and described what he could not see. Then we went to the old meetinghouse where his great-grandfather had been an elder. My visitor was grateful, almost overwhelmed.

There was only one more thing he wanted. Hesitantly, he said, "My grandmother was such a wonderful lady, a Christian lady. Is there a way . . . could you . . . forgive her?" I had no precedent but I did not hesitate. We bowed in prayer, and in the name of the Church of the Brethren I reclaimed a long lost sister.

—*Jim Benedict, Union Bridge, Maryland*

Kline's Meetinghouse, Indian Creek congregation, built in 1843. BHLA Collection.

Council Meeting June 11. 1903.
meeting opened by singing and prayer
and reading of Col. 3.
1st The report of the visit on the
south side was given, Bros Bratten
and Rohrer made the visit and
report peace and union existing
between all the members, some
complaint was made in regard to
members following the fashions of
the world. Elder Eisenbise gave a
good admonition in regard to
those things.
Bro Slifer and wife made the visit
on the north side. Bro Slifer reports
all the members in love and union
A collection was taken for expense
of the love feast and $16.10 was raised
Bro Slifer presented a bill of $3.75
for repairing the furnace in the
grove house, the bill was accepted.

Deacons traveled in pairs before love feast to visit each family in the congregation. In these minutes from the Arnold's Grove church in Illinois, deacons report back to the congregation that everything is in order in the north half and the south half of the territory and love feast can proceed. In rare cases, love feast was postponed until the congregation was unified. BHLA Collection.

One thing that would happen years ago sometimes is that people would be turned away from the table. In the time I was growing up, there was still church discipline, and so there were reasons that you were not permitted to take communion. Generally that was taken care of before communion. You had the annual visit, called the deacons visit, and usually a couple of weeks before communion you would have the special council meeting where the deacons would report what they found on the annual visit. Among these, of course, were certain cases where disciplinary action was taken and certain people were, as they said years ago, set back from communion.

The Brethren had two orders of excommunication. One was full excommunication for a major transgression, when a person was stubborn and would not repent (as they say, make his things right) and you were totally cut off from the fellowship. That was full excommunication or, in German, *absonderung*. The lesser excommunication was called literally "to be set back from the table" or *zurichstellt vom disch*. Until you confessed and were absolved, you would not be permitted to take communion, and you were also not to be given the holy kiss during that period. You were cut off from the kiss and communion.

There were times when people were obstinate and decided they were going to go to the communion table anyway and the elders would have to tell them they were not welcome at the table, unless they made their peace with brethren and sisters. I remember that happening once in my time, but my parents and the older people remember that it would happen from time to time.

—*Clarence Kulp, Harleysville, Pennsylvania*

1880 Council Meeting April 6th 1880
Reading of 4 chap Ephesians by Wm Eisenbise
certificates handed in and read before the church
Sister Emma Mentz from Yellow Creek Stepheson Co.
Ill. Abut Kinney and wife from Hickory Grove
Carroll Co. Ills. Certificates granted Benjamin
Kingery & wife, Susan Taylor (wife of Bro Jas. Taylor)
Sister Lizzie Kinney (wife Bro. Kinney)

Bro Calvin Mummert is bought to (1880
account about signing his Father's name to
a Note without his consent. Calvin committed
this wrong during his expulsion from the Church
He says at the time he signed it he did not
mean to do wrong and intended to pay the Note
without making his Father any trouble, but before
the note is paid Calvin becomes a cripple through
sickness. consequently his Father has to see that
the note is paid. Samuel Mummert complains
to some of the brethren about Calvin's actions.
The Church demands of Bro Calvin. to make an
humble acknowledgement to the church, and also
to his Father. and to do all in his power to
help his him to pay the Note. Also to acknowledge
for some rash expressions he made before the church
this morning. And Calvin is to stay from the
communion table until the Note difficulty is cleared up
Certificate of membership read before the Church
of John Smith and May Ann his wife from
Milledgeville Church Carroll Co Ills.
The Church agrees to pay Wm Slifer $20. for
1 year for acting as Sexton

Calvin Mummert's problem was discovered during the annual deacon visit and was brought before the congregation at council meeting. As was customary, the congregation asks him to "sit back from the table" until his difficulty is cleared up. His absence will mean that the congregation can consider itself otherwise unified and ready for love feast. *BHLA Collection.*

32

The examination sermon was followed by a visit to each family by the deacons, of whom there were six in Baugo, who traveled in pairs like the disciples of old. Before beginning their visitation they met with Grandfather. Exactly what was said I never learned, but I can guess. Each Baugo member's record was examined and the deacons were encouraged not to shrink from their duty.

My father was one of the deacons; so he was usually out on a visitation trip with his partner, Dave Holmes, when Eli Wenger and Delbert Markham stopped at our house. We knew about what time to expect them; so mother had washed our faces. My sisters and I had put on clean clothes. If the hired man were a member of the church, he joined the family circle. Mother met the deacons at the door, greeted them, and invited them to be seated.

For several minutes all sat stiff and silent. Eli Wenger was short and fat and slow-spoken. Delbert Markham was old and stooped, his gray beard scraggly and unkempt. Both men were none too happy at their task. For forty years two sharp-tongued and efficient deaconesses had told them what to say—and now they were alone. But the questioning could not be postponed indefinitely.

Delbert looked at Eli and Eli turned to Mother. "Sister Eby, are you still in the same faith as on the day of your baptism?" Mother nodded affirmatively. Eli continued, "Are you at peace with the brethren?" Mother usually was. "Do you have any suggestions for the advancement of the Kingdom? Anything you wish to have righted before communion?" Mother hadn't. She was thinking of the bread in the oven or the chicks that needed penning up before the threatening rain fell. Finding all in order, Eli and Delbert said good-by until next communion time.

—*Kermit Eby,* For Brethren Only, *1958*

Congregations or the architects they hired gave little attention to the central liturgical act for Brethren—the love feast. This was often relegated to the basement or all-purpose fellowship hall. Some congregations used removable shelves across the back of benches in the main worship room, permitting what one wag called "back of the neck" love feasts. Earlier meetinghouses of the nineteenth century had designed ingenious benches with pivoted backs that could be converted into tables for the love feast ordinance.

—*Donald F. Durnbaugh,* Fruit of the Vine

In some meetinghouses, such as Middle Creek in Pennsylvania, the pews were transformed into tables by clamping a plank atop every other pew.
Middle Creek Congregational Archives.

The Dunker Love-Feast

On the morning of the 25th of September, 1871, I took the cars of the Pennsylvania Central Railroad for the borough of Mount Joy, in the northwest part of this county of Lancaster. Finding no public conveyance thence to the village of C., I obtained from my landlord a horse and buggy and an obliging driver, who took me four or five miles, for two dollars. We took a drive round by the new Dunker meeting-house, which is a neat frame building,—brown, picked out with white window-frames. Behind it is a wood, upon which the church-doors open, instead of upon the highway.

We heard here that the meeting would not begin till one o'clock on the next day. Some of the brethren were at the church, however, with their teams, having brought provisions, straw, and bedding. We went into the neat meeting-room, and above into the garret, where straw was being laid down. A partition ran down the middle, and upon the women's side a small room had also been divided from the rest, wherein were one or two bedsteads and the inevitable cradle. The basement had a hard earthen floor, and was divided into dining-room, kitchen, and cellar. Upon spacious shelves in the cellar a brother and sister were placing food. Many large loaves of bread were there. The sister was taking pies from a great basket, and bright coffee-pots stood upon the kitchen-table.

All here seemed to speak "Dutch," but several talked English with me.

Before meetinghouses were built, congregations cleared out large spaces in barns for worship and love feast. This old farm near the Miller's Schoolhouse in Pennsylvania was the site of many love feasts. BHLA Collection.

As a girl, one thing I did not anticipate joyfully was the annual "deacons' visit" prior to the love feast. At the Indian Creek church, both ministers and deacons helped in these visits. Two men were paired together to make the visits. It seemed to me to be a stiff, formal occasion. It made me somewhat uncomfortable. As I recall it, each of us in turn was asked such questions as whether we remained in the faith we had when we were baptized; whether we were still "in love and fellowship with the Brethren"; whether we had anything against a "brother" or "sister" in the church or knew of anything that anyone had against us; and whether we had any concerns to be brought up at the council meeting. Sometimes my father had a suggestion for something to be included in the council business. A prayer ended the visit. I must admit feeling relieved when the visit was over for another year!

—*Gladys Mease, Goshen, Indiana*

They seemed surprised that I had come so far as twenty-three miles in order to attend the meeting. One remarked that it was no member that had put the notice of the meeting which I had seen into the paper. Others, however, seemed interested, although by my dress it was very plain that I was not of the brotherhood.

. . . the [next] morning having proved wet, a neighbor took me over to the church in his buggy for twenty-five cents. Although the hour was so early, and meeting was fixed to begin at one, I found a considerable number here, which did not surprise me, as I knew the early habits of our "Dutch" people. Taking a seat, I began to read a number of the *Living Age*, when a black-eyed maid before me, in Dunker dress, handed me her neatly-bound hymn-book in English and German. I told her that I could read German, and when I read a verse in that language she said, "But you don't know what it means." Reading German is with us a much rarer accomplishment than speaking the dialect.

Ere long, a stranger came and sat down behind me, and entered into conversation. He was a preacher from a distance named L., and spoke very good English. We soon found that we had mutual acquaintances in another county, and when dinner was ready he invited me down to partake.

Here the men sat upon one side, and the women on the other, of one of the long tables, upon which was laid a strip of white muslin. We had bowls without spoons, into which was poured by attending brethren very hot coffee, containing milk or cream, but no sugar. We had the fine Lancaster County bread, good and abundant butter, apple-butter, pickles, and pies. The provisions for these meals are contributed by the members at a previous meeting, where each tells what he intends to furnish, how many loaves of bread, etc., while some prefer to give money. To furnish provisions, however, is natural to a people of whom about seventy-five in a hundred are farmers, as is the case with the Dunkers. Whatever food is left over after the four meals are finished is given to the poor, without distinction of sect; "whoever needs it most," as a sister said. . . .

When we went up into the meeting-room again, a young man of an interesting countenance, a preacher, named Z., asked me if I was not the one who had written an article which had lately appeared in one of our county papers. It was very gratifying to be thus recognized among strangers.

An elderly sister, who sat down by me and began to talk, was named Murphy. The name surprised me much, but it was not the only Irish one here. It is probably that some such persons were taken into Dunker families, when young, to be brought up, and thus had been led to join the society. Having observed that there was a good deal of labor to be performed here in waiting upon so many people, I asked Mrs. Murphy whether there were women hired. She told me, "There's a couple of women that's hired; but the members does a heap, too."

On another occasion, I made a remark to a friendly sister about the brethren's waiting upon the table, as they did. She answered that it was according to the Testament to help each other; the women cooked and the men waited upon the table. She did not seem able to give the text. It may be, "Bear ye one another's burdens." I was amused that it should be so kindly applied to the brethren's helping the sisters.

Before meeting began in the afternoon, a lovely aged brother, with silvery hair and beard, and wearing a woolen coat nearly white, showed me how the seats were made, so that, by turning down the backs of some, tables could be formed for the Love-Feast. . . .

When meeting began, as brethren came in, I saw some of these bearded men kissing each other. These holy kisses, as will be seen hereafter, are frequent among the Dunkers, and, as the men shave only the upper lip, it seems strange to us who are unaccustomed to the sight and the sound. The oft-repeated kissing was to me, perhaps, the least agreeable part of the ceremonial.

Women's prayer coverings were standard dress, at least for worship and love feast, until the middle twentieth century. A few sisters still wear them today. Some congregations provide prayer coverings at love feast for visitors or those who forget theirs. Regina Bryan photo.

The afternoon meeting became very crowded, and, as is usual among our "Dutch " people, a number of babies were in attendance. During the sessions their voices sometimes rose high, but the noise did not seem to affect those who were preaching or praying. They felt it perhaps like the wailing and sighing of the wind, which they regard not, and would rather bear the inconvenience of the children than to have the mothers stay away from meeting. This afternoon, during prayer, a little fellow behind me kept saying, "Want to go to pappy"; but if his father was among the brethren, he was on the other side of the house.

My new acquaintance, L., was the only preacher here who spoke in English. All the other exercises, except a little singing, were in German or in our Pennsylvania dialect. This afternoon L. said, among many remarks more sectarian, or less broad, "Faith is swallowed up in sight; hope, in possession; but charity, or love, is eternal. It came from God, for God is love." The allusion here is to Paul's celebrated pane-gyric on charity; but how much more charming it is in the German version, "Faith, hope, love; but the greatest of these is love. Love suffereth long and is kind, is not puffed up," etc. . . . .

During the interval of the election I sat and read, or looked out from my window at the young people, the gayly-dressed girls mostly grouped together. Some of these were, probably, relatives of the members, while others may have come for the ride and the fun, to see and to be seen,—meetings of this kind being great occasions in the country-side.

The young men stood around on the outside of these groups of girls, some holding their whips and twirling them, with the butts resting upon the ground. Of course the young girls were not conscious of the presence of the beaux.

. . . a nice-looking woman . . . wore the plain cap. "Most of the women do around here," she said, and added that Dunker women in meeting had offered to kiss her. "You know they greet each other with a kiss. . . ."

Typical nineteenth-century dress for women included a prayer covering that covered the head completely and tied under the chin. By the mid-twentieth century, prayer coverings were small and rested on top of the head.
Photo loaned by Esther Austin, Bloomington, Indiana.

41

Psalm 139:7-12, 23-24

Where can I go from your spirit?
>   Or where can I flee from your presence?
If I ascend to heaven, you are there;
>   if I make my bed in Sheol, you are there.
If I take the wings of the morning
>   and settle at the farthest limits of the sea,
even there your hand shall lead me,
>   and your right hand shall hold me fast.
If I say, "Surely the darkness shall cover me,
>   and the light around me become night,"
even the darkness is not dark to you;
>   the night is as bright as the day,
>   for darkness is as light to you.

Search me, O God, and know my heart;
>   test me and know my thoughts.
See if there is any wicked way in me,
>   and lead me in the way everlasting.

As sunset approached, some of the members began to form tables from the benches for the Love-Feast, which made me wonder when supper was to be ready. I soon found, however, that my ignorance of the language had prevented my observing that while the "family" voted the rest of the congregation were to sup. I was told, however, that if I could go down I could still get something to eat. These meals were free to every one that came. All were received, in the hope that they would obtain some spiritual good.

In the basement I found a number of men sitting at the end of one of the tables, waiting for food, and I also sat down near them. I was invited, however, by a sister to step into the kitchen, where I stood and partook of hot coffee, bread and butter, etc. As we went along through the dining-room, I thought that the sister cast a reproachful glance at a disorderly man seated at the table with his whip, and who was perhaps intoxicated. I wondered that she should have taken me from the table to stand in the kitchen, till I remembered that that was *a men's table*.

In the kitchen, brethren were busily occupied cutting large loaves of bread into quarters for the coming Love-Feast; and when I returned to the room above, active preparations were still going on, which consumed much time. The improvised tables were neatly covered with white cloths, and hanging lamps shed down light upon the scene. Piles of tin pans were placed upon the table, knives, forks, and spoons, and sometimes a bowl. The tables, with their seats, occupied nearly the whole floor of the church, leaving but little room for spectators. I was myself crowded into a corner, where the stairs came up from the basement and went up to the loft; but, though at times I was much pressed for room, I had an excellent place to observe, for I stood at the end of the main table. Here stood, too, a bright and social sister from a neighboring congregation, who did not partake of the feast, and was able and willing to explain the ceremonial to me, in English,—Mrs. R., as I will call her.

Typical nineteenth-century dress for men included a broad brimmed hat, plain coat (no lapels), full beard, and no mustache. BHLA Collection.

43

Command your angles to serve
and fill us now with good manners,
let them be seated around us
so that nothing may transpire that disgraces this table.

—*"Ach Herr Jesu," from the first Brethren hymnal,*
  Geistreiches Gesang-Buch, *1720*

Near by at the table, among the older sisters, sat a pair who attracted a great deal of my attention—a young mother and her babe—herself so quiet, and such a quiet babe! They might have been photographed. Once or twice the little six-weeks' child gave a feeble young wail, and I saw the youthful mother modestly give it that nourishment which nature provides.

The brethren came up carrying tubs of meat, which smelt savory, for I had fasted from flesh since the morning. Then came great vessels of soup,—one of them a very large tin wash-boiler. The soup was taken out into the tin pans before mentioned, and the plates of meat were set upon the top, as if to keep both hot. And, now . . . "at long last" the Love-Feast tables were spread.

—*from articles and essays by Phebe E. Gibbons, nineteenth-century journalist*

Graydon Snyder Collection.

Youth: Why is this night different from all other nights? Why is eating such a central part of our worship tonight? At other times of evening worship we eat a carry-in meal before or after the service. And why are we so quiet as we eat?

Pastor: Tonight we remember the meal Jesus ate with his disciples on the night before his death. We also celebrate the community created in the Christ event. Our silence and hushed whispers are in reverence for this powerful story and its meaning for our lives.

Youth: Why do we take time to examine our hearts and confess our sins before we eat? Normally we only offer a prayer to thank God for the food or sing a favorite table grace before eating. Why must we take so much more time tonight?

Pastor: The meal we share tonight is held in honor of our Lord Jesus Christ. It is a celebration of the gathered faith community, so we need to examine our hearts to make sure we are in proper relationship with God and our brothers and sisters. If those relationships are broken, it is time to repair them.

Our brother Paul warned us not to eat this meal in an unworthy manner. He said we would bring judgment upon ourselves if we did (1 Cor. 11:27-32). Our eating together is an act of worship. Jesus says that we must be in right relationship with one another before we can offer our worship to God.

—For All Who Minister

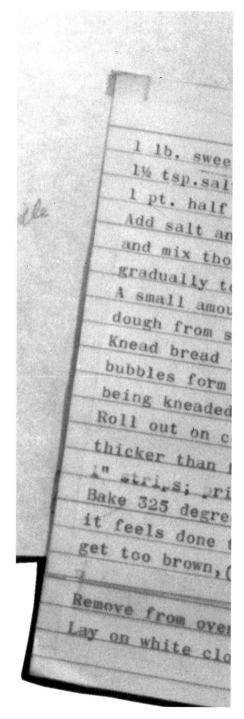

1. S. C. and B. Ulrey and Phebe Weaver recd by letter.

2. J. Prisers report on missionery fund.

Paid	Benj Neff	$19.40
"	Sol Ockerman	8.66
"	tract work	3.65
"	Hund Pa for Bible Lessons	1.60
"	Tract work	1.58
Money on hand		.05
		$34.96

3. Priser's report accepted by the church and he agreed to serve as solicitor until Aug 1/4 C. M. 1889.

4. Jos Ulrey's report of 1887 (church treas.).

Money laid in the for Communion	$43.28
Money laid in since the communion	$ 4.25
	47.53

Paid for the beef for commun.			460 lbs	$29.60
"	"	"	coffee "	25 lbs	5.50
"	"	"	sugar "	20 lbs	1.20
"	"	"	Tea "	1 "	.50
"	"	"	Wine "	1 gal	2.00
"	"	"	coal oil "	2 "	.25
					$39.05

Sold after communion	Butter	3.62
	coffee	1.10
	Tea	.12
	sugar	.36
	Beef	1.00
	Total	**6.20**

Cash 47.53,   Articles sold 6.20   Total $53.73

Paid for redressing butter	$ .75
" " tending horses	1.00
" " washing table cloths	1.50
" " 3 sets knives & forks	1.50
" " 1 doz. Spoons	.25
" " 1 tub	.35
" " 3 lamp flues	.50
" " bolts and nails	.42
" " 6 lamps	2.30
" " 1 gal oil	.15
" " 5 lamp flues	.46
" " 2 brooms	.40
" " 2 baskets	.10
" " in cash to the church	5.00
	$14.68

Articles bought for the communion $39.05 and articles bought for the church $14.68, total of $53.13.

—Eel River Church Council Meeting minutes, November 3, 1888

Recipes for the meal and communion and instructions on conducting the love feast are handed down from generation to generation of deacons. Pictured between these recipes is a chart for setting up tables for love feast. Regina Bryan photo.

I remember the atmosphere when the visiting Brethren were coming. They would make an appointment with my parents and there was just a sense of heightened anticipation that the visiting Brethren were coming. I remember an automobile pulling into the lot, so my father'd turn over the store business to one of the old men visiting, and we'd go to the other side of the house, which was our dwelling, and sit in the parlor, and my father would go to the door and the two brothers would come in and they would sit down and perhaps for ten or fifteen minutes, maybe even a little more, they would just talk, about the community, about the weather, whatever would come up in conversation.

Then usually the older of the two would say, "Now brother and sister, you know the business we are here to conduct and we should get down to our business." Then they would usually talk a little bit about the importance of the spiritual significance of the love feast communion, and they would ask my parents the three questions.

First of all, they'd say, "Are you in the faith as you were when you accepted Christ in baptism?" They'd turn to my father and he would give assent, then turn to my mother and she would nod or say yes.

And then they would say, "Are you, as far as lies with you, living at peace with all men, especially with the brethren and sisters? Again they would give their assent.

And then finally the third question was, "Are you resolved to continue to work together with the brethren and sisters at this place, to be obedient to the will of God in your lives?" Again they'd give their assent. Then he would ask whether they had any exhortation, any concern, they wanted to send along to the special precommunion council meeting. If they did he would make a note of it, or if not he would say, "Now before we go we want to have prayer." We'd all kneel down in the parlor, usually both brethren would pray, usually the younger one would pray first, a shorter prayer, and then the older man would say a longer prayer and then close with the Lord's Prayer. Then they'd get up and they'd greet my father with the kiss of peace and shake hand with my mother and they'd always shake hand with me and then we'd go back into the store and resume our regular duties, but it was, I remember, always a very impressive thing. I mean we would go to meeting every Sunday morning, but this was the church coming to you, coming into your home, and there was just something special about it.

—*Clarence Kulp, Harleysville, Pennsylvania*

Deacons and circuit riders such as this minister traveled great distances through the district or region on horseback.

Now during those days, when the disciples were increasing in number, the Hellenists complained against the Hebrews because their widows were being neglected in the daily distribution of food. And the twelve called together the whole community of the disciples and said, "It is not right that we should neglect the word of God in order to wait on tables. Therefore, friends, select from among yourselves seven men of good standing, full of the Spirit and of wisdom, whom we may appoint to this task, while we, for our part, will devote ourselves to prayer and to serving the word."

What they said pleased the whole community, and they chose Stephen, a man full of faith and the Holy Spirit, together with Philip, Prochorus, Nicanor, Timon, Parmenas, and Nicolaus, a proselyte of Antioch. They had these men stand before the apostles, who prayed and laid their hands on them.

—*Acts 6:1-6*

Whoever, therefore, eats the bread or drinks the cup of the Lord
in an unworthy manner will be answerable for the body and blood
of the Lord. Examine yourselves, and only then eat of the bread
and drink of the cup. For all who eat and drink without discerning
the body, eat and drink judgment against themselves. For this reason
many of you are weak and ill, and some have died. But if we judged
ourselves, we would not be judged. But when we are judged by the
Lord, we are disciplined so that we may not be condemned along
with the world.

So then, my brothers and sisters, when you come together to eat,
wait for one another. If you are hungry, eat at home, so that when you
come together, it will not be for your condemnation. About the other
things I will give instructions when I come.

—1 Corinthians 11:27-34

Jeanine Wine

Now while Jesus was at Bethany in the house of Simon the leper, a woman came to him with an alabaster jar of very costly ointment, and she poured it on his head as he sat at the table. But when the disciples saw it, they were angry and said, "Why this waste? For this ointment could have been sold for a large sum, and the money given to the poor." But Jesus, aware of this, said to them, "Why do you trouble the woman? She has performed a good service for me. For you always have the poor with you, but you will not always have me. By pouring this ointment on my body she has prepared me for burial. Truly I tell you, wherever this good news is proclaimed in the whole world, what she has done will be told in remembrance of her."

—*Matthew 26:6-13*

FEETWASHING

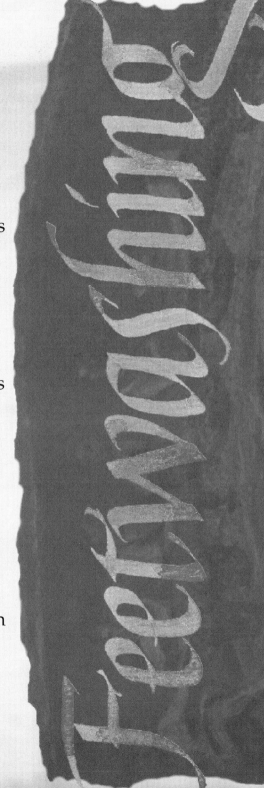

Now before the festival of the Passover, Jesus knew that his hour had come to depart from this world and go to the Father. Having loved his own who were in the world, he loved them to the end. The devil had already put it into the heart of Judas son of Simon Iscariot to betray him. And during supper Jesus, knowing that the Father had given all things into his hands, and that he had come from God and was going to God, got up from the table, took off his outer robe, and tied a towel around himself. Then he poured water into a basin and began to wash the disciples' feet and to wipe them with the towel that was tied around him.

—John 13:1-5

EETWASHING in the ancient world was primarily performed by slaves. People of all ages in subservient positions could be required to wash feet and have no choice in the matter.

Washing feet was necessary. The roads were dusty, and among the layers of dirt was fecal matter from pack animals. Even with sandals a person arrived with dirty feet. It was customary to wash before visiting someone, but when guests arrived at the home of the host, only the feet were considered dirty. Servants (or the wife of the host) washed the guests' feet as a sign of hospitality.

There are a few examples in the ancient world, both in and beyond biblical texts, of people voluntarily choosing to wash the feet of a superior as a symbol of hospitality, fealty, or love. But according to scholar John Christopher Thomas, there is no example prior to Jesus of a master washing the feet of his inferiors. Thomas believes that Peter at first mistook the action of Jesus for such an act of hospitality. As the guest in the upper room, Jesus ordinarily would not have been the one to do the washing. However, Jesus was performing this act as a servant, not as a guest.

The early church understood the meaning of Jesus' action. There is plenty of evidence in ancient Christian writings that believers took the words of Jesus literally; in various settings, both in and out of the communion service, they washed each other's feet. This action continued well past the legalization of Christianity.

Clearly, feetwashing is uncomfortable, perhaps even untenable, for many Christians. That may explain why even most biblical literalists do not interpret this passage literally. As Brethren Bible scholar Vernard Eller points out in *In Place of Sacraments*,

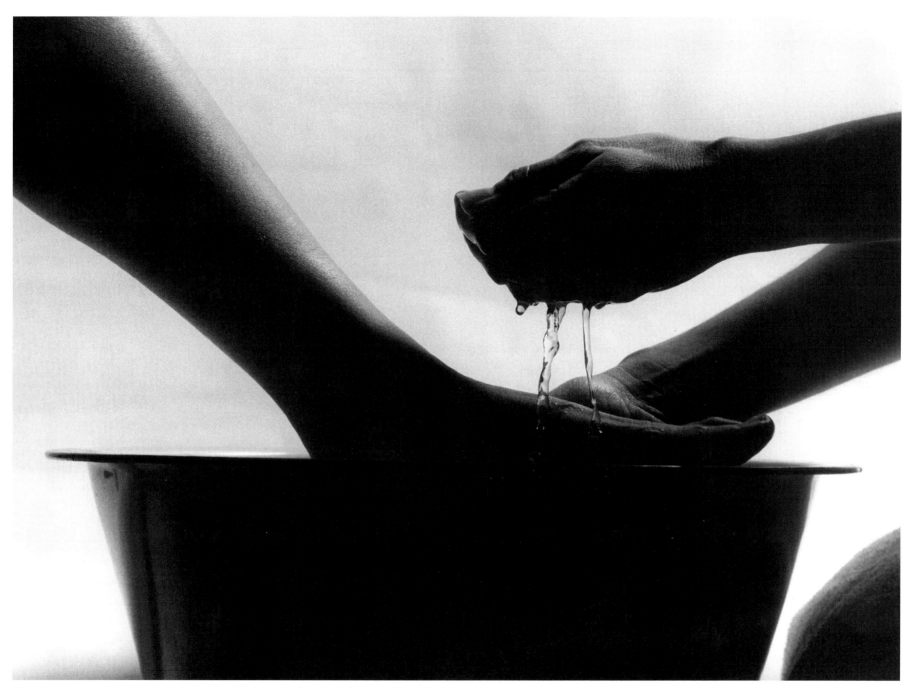

"For I have set you an example, that you also should do as I have done to you" (John 13:15). Photo by Phil Grout.

Truth to tell, the command regarding feetwashing is clearer and more decisive than the command regarding the bread and cup.

—*Vernard Eller,* In Place of Sacraments

Granted, there are some people (even among the Brethren, whose Supper has always included feetwashing) who demur on the grounds that the very act of baring one's own feet or of washing another's is distasteful and impolite. Their argument is that feetwashing was an accepted custom in Jesus' day but one that is completely foreign to us. Nevertheless, it must be recalled that Jesus chose to wash the disciples' feet precisely *because* of the offense and scandal involved. It is true that the offense was not related to delicate feelings about bare feet; it came at a much deeper, a much more scandalous level, and one we hardly are in position to appreciate. Yes, feet were publicly washed in Jesus' day—but no one but slaves were expected to do it. Jesus washed feet as a way of demonstrating that he was willing to make himself a slave out of love for his brethren. It is certain that he did not do it for the sake of any pleasurable sensations involved. And Peter's response, "I will never let you wash my feet," indicates something of the shock he felt. Thank God feet washing is still somewhat distasteful; otherwise we would miss the point entirely. (112-113)

Though feetwashing was commonly practiced in Christianity through the fourth century, few groups practice feetwashing as part of the Lord's Supper anymore. The Brethren, however, finding the practice of feetwashing together with the *agape* meal and the eucharist in John, practice all three in obedience to scripture. In their quest to live out the biblical mandate, however, several question have plagued the Brethren, for instance: Should disciples wash feet before or after the meal? Should one or two people wash everyone's feet around the table (double mode), or should a disciple wash the feet of the next person, who washes the feet of the next person, and so on around the table (single mode)? Must the sexes separate, or can they wash one another's feet? Can Christians who are not Brethren participate in the ordinance?

One of the first controversies regarding the love feast was in the order of the ordinances. Should feetwashing take place after or before the meal?

In the late eighteenth century, Alexander Mack Jr. (1712–1803) wrote about a controversy among the eastern Pennsylvania Brethren on the correct timing of the feetwashing service. Because of the scriptural account of

Prayer of Ambrose

Come then, Lord Jesus. . . . Pour water into the basin, wash not only our feet but also the head and not only the body, but also the footsteps of the soul. I wish to put off all filth of our frailty. Wash the steps of my mind that I may not sin again. Wash the heel of my soul, that I may be able to efface the curse, that I feel not the serpent's bite on the foot of my soul, but as Thou Thyself has bidden those who follow Thee, may tread on serpents and scorpions with uninjured foot.

—*"Of the Holy Spirit," 1.13,* Nicene and Post-Nicene Fathers

Close up of a fifth-century sarcophagus at Arles depicting Jesus washing the disciples' feet. So deep was the shame of the cross that it took five hundred years before that brutal method of execution was included in authentic Christian art. And the demand Jesus made of his disciples that they model his humility by taking on the aspect of a slave in feet-washing was so profound that this too does not appear in Christian art for nearly five centuries. Graydon Snyder Collection.

"I, your Lord and Master, have
Washed your feet, and also gave
The command that ye should do
As I now have done to you."

Teach the world, and practice, too,
Each command I gave to you;
By this then shall all men see,
Who my true disciples be.
—A Collection of Hymns
  and Sacred Songs

Jesus rising from supper to perform this (John 13:2-4), some believed that feetwashing should be observed following the meal and before the breaking of bread. Mack responded that in his experience Brethren had washed feet *after* the meal and the breaking of the bread, *after* the meal and *before* the breaking of bread, and currently *before* the meal and breaking of bread. For his part, he averred that

> if a brother or any other person can in love and moderation instruct us according to the word of the Lord more fully and otherwise than is here pointed out, we should be ready to accept of it not only in this point of feetwashing but also in other matters, and not at all rest on long usage, but let the word of the Lord be our only rule and guide.

Mack pointed out that Christ did not reveal that his disciples would be known by the manner of washing of feet or breaking of bread, but rather through this word: "By this everyone will know that you are my disciples, if you have love for one another" (John 13:35). He concluded with an admonition that has been meaningful for many through the years: "Therefore, dear brethren, let us watch and be careful. *Above all let us preserve love, for then we will preserve light.* Then our great God, who is love purely and impartially, can and will add by degrees what may be wanting in this or that knowledge of truth" [emphasis added]. Whether the question involves the Lord's Supper or anything else, this admonition by Alexander Mack Jr. can be commended to us all. (Donald Durnbaugh, *The Lord's Supper: Believers Church Perspectives*, 78)

The same forbearance was needed on other issues as well. When Jesus said "you also ought to wash one another's feet," he didn't say clearly whether one person should wash all, or whether each person should wash the next person's feet in turn. And since only men were present for the first feetwashing, there is no guidance in the Gospel of John on the participation of women. From time to time, Brethren have struggled with proper interpretation of scripture, but on the whole they have been willing to change if the Holy Spirit leads them to new and better thinking on an issue. In the case of double- and single-mode feetwashing, the body slowly diverged in its practice and then slowly converged on the single mode (washing in turn), based on the method employed at the first love feast in Pennsylvania, 1723.

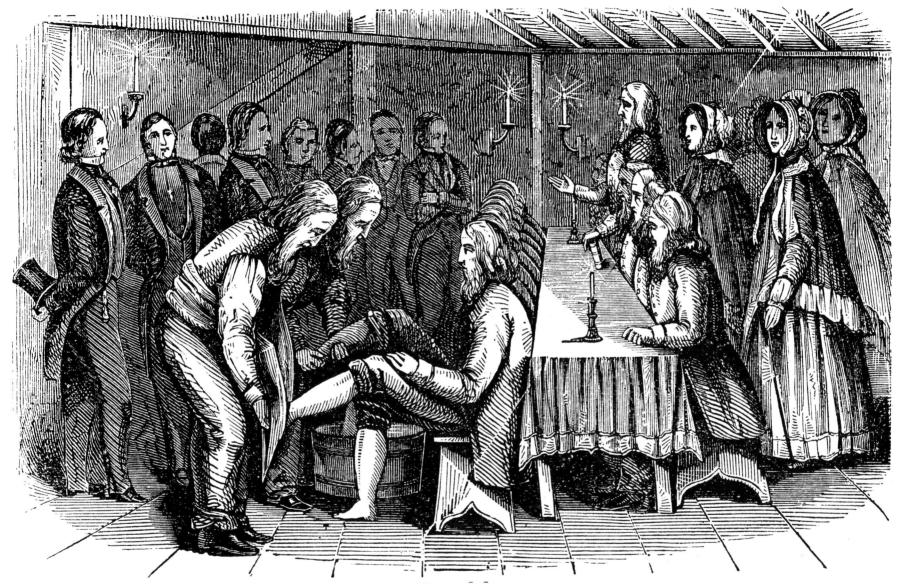

While the ritual of feetwashing was limited to members, curious onlookers were permitted to watch the ordinance from the edges. In this drawing by G. L. Croome, onlookers at the far right and left are distinguished from members by their worldly clothing. Published in Peter Nead's Theological Writings, 1850.

German journalist Moritz Busch, while visiting America in 1851, witnessed a Brethren love feast and wrote regarding one of the preachers:

> He must have spoken about a half-hour in this fashion, when his sermon took a characteristic turn as he suddenly abandoned the lame in the temple at Jerusalem, forgot his English, and in the purest Pennsylvania Dutch complained about the pain in his lungs: "I could talk much longer on this text, but my lungs won't stand it. Oh, my lungs! But however . . ." and then the flow of words poured forth well over another quarter of an hour without period or pause, in its rise and fall similar to that in which we sing the collect [in German churches].

—*Donald Durnbaugh,* Fruit of the Vine

The single and double modes of feetwashing

By all accounts the Germantown congregation, affectionately called the "mother church," practiced feetwashing by the so-called "single mode." As is the practice today, a brother or sister would wash the feet of the brother or sister next to him or her, and that person would wash the feet of the next person, and so on, but the Conestoga church, under the leadership of Conrad Beissel, began to practice the "double mode." Two brothers or sisters would proceed down a row of believers, one washing and the other drying feet. After awhile the two would be relieved by another set of two, who would continue the practice.

A number of congregations sprang from the Conestoga church. Soon nearly all of the Brethren congregations in Pennsylvania, Virginia, and along the eastern seaboard were practicing the double mode, except the Germantown congregation, and a few isolated churches.

Despite the pervasiveness of the double mode at that time, Brethren moving westward in search of land and opportunity took with them the original practice of the Brethren. These "far western" Brethren, located in Kansas and the Midwest, observed the single mode of feetwashing and the practice of allowing sisters to break bread for themselves. Time and travel being what they were, the far western group became separated from eastern and southern Brethren. But in 1856, after much debate regarding feetwashing, these Brethren were received back into the larger fellowship. It was agreed that everyone would practice "forbearance" until the church came to some unity on the question.

In 1859 representatives of the far western Brethren agreed to let Annual Meeting have the final say in the matter, but even after Annual Meeting called for the double mode, the practice of the single mode did not cease in the West. Indeed, it continued to spread. As far as the eastern Brethren were concerned, something had to be done. Once the Civil War was over and the task of keeping the Brethren united on both sides of the Mason-Dixon Line was accomplished, the elders of the church could turn their attention back to the more important matter of maintaining order. The 1871 Annual Meeting formed such a committee whose most important member was D. P. Sayler,

Late twentieth-century love feast at Germantown Church of the Brethren (Pennsylvania). Video image by David Sollenberger.

Now before the festival of the Passover, Jesus knew that his hour had come to depart from this world and go to the Father. Having loved his own who were in the world, he loved them to the end. The devil had already put it into the heart of Judas son of Simon Iscariot to betray him. And during supper Jesus, knowing that the Father had given all things into his hands, and that he had come from God and was going to God, got up from the table, took off his outer robe, and tied a towel around himself. Then he poured water into a basin and began to wash the disciples' feet and to wipe them with the towel that was tied around him. He came to Simon Peter, who said to him, "Lord, are you going to wash my feet?" Jesus answered, "You do not know now what I am doing, but later you will understand." Peter said to him, "You will never wash my feet." Jesus answered, "Unless I wash you, you have no share with me." Simon Peter said to him, "Lord, not my feet only but also my hands and my head!" Jesus said to him, "One who has bathed does not need to wash, except for the feet, but is entirely clean. And you are clean, though not all of you." For he knew who was to betray him; for this reason he said, "Not all of you are clean."

After he had washed their feet, had put on his robe, and had returned to the table, he said to them, "Do you know what I have done to you? You call me Teacher and Lord—and you are right, for that is what I am. So if I, your Lord and Teacher, have washed your feet, you also ought to wash one another's feet. For I have set you an example, that you also should do as I have done to you. Very truly, I tell you, servants are not greater than their master, nor are messengers greater than the one who sent them. If you know these things, you are blessed if you do them."

—John 13:1-17

The holy kiss was often commanded by Jesus (Rom. 16:16; 1 Cor. 16:20, and elsewhere) as an expression of the love that should exist between members of the church. Besides the solid scriptural authority, Brethren found the practice documented for the early church (Acts 20:37) and by early church fathers such as Justin Martyr and Cyprian. As has been seen, the ordinance was an important element in the full love feast. Brethren also observed the practice, separated by gender, when meeting in homes and in public gathering for worship. Conversely, withholding the kiss was used in church discipline to indicate estrangement.

—*Donald Durnbaugh,* Fruit of the Vine

one of the leading Brethren authorities of the time.

There is much good to be said about Sayler, but he had one blind spot, and that was the single mode of feetwashing. Sayler's two basic arguments were that the Germantown church was not the mother church, but a "sister" to the Conestoga church, which had priority and which practiced the double mode. In addition he pointed to a passage in the *Ephrata Chronicles* which seemed to support the notion that the double mode was practiced by the ancient church.

The *Ephrata Chronicles* came from the Ephrata Cloisters, which were founded by mystic and Brethren separatist Conrad Beisel. Not having found anyone worthy to baptize him, Beisel renounced his earlier baptisms and baptized himself. The cloisters he founded are a rich part of Pennsylvania history and had a deep, if difficult, impact on the early Brethren, as families were sometimes split over joining Beisel's venture. However, the reference that Sayler prized describes a feetwashing conducted by Beisel and an associate for two visitors, and was not part of a worship service.

Eventually, in the 1880s, the single mode was reestablished based in part on the historical evidence culled from Abraham Harley Cassel's library of ancient Brethren documents, which documented the single mode as the original method.

The holy kiss

As uncomfortable as feetwashing is to some, it is only mildly awkward compared to "the salutation" or holy kiss. In general, when all had washed and been washed, a kiss was passed from man to man, woman to woman, around the room, the last person coming around to the beginning to kiss the first woman or man. When the kiss came full circle around both halves of the room, the body was unified. In most cases today, the kiss (or a brush of the cheeks) and the peace of Christ are passed after the servant has washed and dried the feet of a brother or sister, removed the towel, and tied it to his or her neighbor's waist.

Numerous queries came to district meetings and Annual Meeting asking permission to forego the kiss between men when brothers chewed tobacco or kept untrimmed beards that became encrusted with food or frost. Also, in

G. L. Croome Del.

The holy kiss is a sign of unity among Brethren. G. L. Croome's drawing, published in Peter Nead's Theological Writings, shows the kiss as a greeting between members. In the order of the love feast, the kiss is shared after feetwashing.

Though Annual Meeting declared that "we make no difference on account of race or color," Samuel Weir, a freed slave who became a licensed Brethren minister and elder in black congregations in Ohio, suffered the prejudices of white members and was denied membership in some congregations.
Drawing by Kermon Thomasson (BHLA Collection).

1835 a query came to Annual Meeting asking whether Brethren should receive Negroes into membership, to which the answer was: "Considered, to make no difference on account of color." Another query asked if Negro members should be treated the same as white members, this being a thinly veiled request to abstain from the salutation with people of another race. The answer to this query was,

> It was considered, that inasmuch as the gospel is to be preached to all nations and races, and if they come as repentant sinners, believing in the gospel of Jesus Christ, and apply for baptism, we could not consistently refuse them. But inasmuch [as] we receive our fellow members with the holy kiss, and there is a repugnance in some of our white members to salute colored persons in this manner, the colored members should bear with that weakness, and not offer the kiss to such weak members until they become stronger, and make the first offer, etc. Otherwise, if they [the colored members] prove faithful, they should be considered on an equality of full membership.

In 1845, the question of membership for Negroes arose again. This time the delegates turned the responsibility for membership guidelines over to individual congregations. "The assembled elders, however, considered [full membership] the more perfect way, to which we should all strive to come, viz., that love, which makes no distinction in the brotherhood, in this respect."

At the root of similar queries in 1849, 1866, 1874, and 1875 was the question of the salutation. The last time the issue came up, a congregation recorded,

> Since the Annual Meeting has left it optional with brethren whether or not to salute colored brethren with the holy kiss, designing men are making capital of it against us. To obviate this, let the Annual Meeting reconsider that decision, and say that we make no difference on account of race or color; and this district-meeting asks the Annual Meeting to make no difference on account of race or color.

In response the Annual Meeting said: "We grant the request, but should have regard to the former minutes of Annual Meeting upon the subject, and

Jesus took a towel

Jesus took a towel and he girded himself,
then he washed my feet, yes, he washed my feet.
Jesus took a basin and he knelt himself down,
and he washed, yes, he washed my feet.

The heavens are the Lord's and the earth is his,
the clouds are his chariot, glory his cloak.
He made the mountains, set the limits of the sea,
and he stooped and washed my feet.

The hour had come, the feast was near;
Jesus loved his own, loved them to the end.
O Lord, let me see, let me understand
why you stooped and washed my feet.

—*Chrysogonus Waddell, O.C.S.O., Copyright © 1968
Gethsemani Abbey, Trappist, Kentucky*

*James May was a convert of Samuel Weir. He held a long tenure
as a minister and elder in Ohio congregations and was briefly a
missionary to blacks in Arkansas.* BHLA Collection.

advise the brethren to bear with one another."

While the record reveals a groundbreaking stand on equality, in practice it was difficult for many congregations to integrate. Former slave Samuel Weir became a member of a white congregation, but when he began to minister in 1872, he ministered only to black congregations. In 1890 James May, a black convert of Samuel Weir, was ordained an elder of a black congregation and continued in ministry, generally to blacks, until his death in 1926. These two leaders demonstrate the distance between the enlightened policy of Annual Meeting and the reality of race relations in the post-Civil War era. Many of these divisions are still to be overcome.

Modern alterations

After a deacon or host begins feetwashing and passes on the foot tub and the peace of Christ, he or she then circulates a small basin and towel for hand washing. But where people have disabilities or objections that make feetwashing difficult or impossible, hand washing is sometimes used as a substitute for the more cumbersome feetwashing. Congregations may also set aside a room for less mobile people who need more time or more privacy. And some Brethren schedule love feast in the afternoon or after Sunday morning worship to minimize nighttime driving for the elderly.

Congregations practice feetwashing in many ways. Sometimes men and women move to separate rooms and wash feet, then come together at tables in a fellowship hall or sanctuary for the *agape* meal and communion. Some congregations wash feet in silence. In others a chorister will lead hymns, sung *a capella*. Some halls are dimly lit by candles. Others are brightly lit as if for any meeting. Some eat sop (beef broth and bread), others eat lamb, some eat cheese sandwiches. But there is remarkable uniformity in the practice of feetwashing. From the hymns, the characteristic towel and basin, the beloved passage from John 13, and most importantly "the love for one another," even a casual observer would know that this is the love feast of the Brethren. *F.R.*

For people who have disabilities that make feetwashing physically difficult, many congregations provide an option for handwashing.

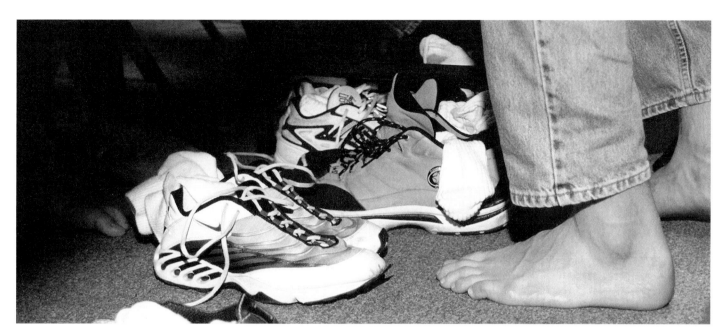

As feetwashing begins, Brethren strip off shoes and socks and await a turn to wash one another's feet.
Photo by Regina Bryan.

At the 1993 conference on ""Ministry to the Sick," sponsored by Johns Hopkins University, I heard Henri Nouwen describe community as the place where the person you least want to live with always is present. You know the feeling; the last person you want to sit next to during love feast or communion always seems to be the person whose feet you end up washing. Community is not a place where no one disagrees. It is the place where forgiveness is more important than being right or wrong, where it is more important to be together in our imperfection than to be alone in our alleged perfection.

—*Dawn Ottoni Wilhelm,* Brethren Life and Thought,
   Spring/Summer 1996

Love Feast Under a Tamarind Tree

In 1943 Mary and I were serving as missionaries in Garkida, Nigeria, where I was in charge of pastoral services and evangelism for a large area. The full New Testament love feast and communion were celebrated four times a year in the Bura language at the central church, and villagers round about walked in for it. But there was a small group of Christians from the Whona tribe about eight miles away, evangelized under Desmond Bittinger, who felt left out. Their language and culture were totally different from others in our mission area, and up to that time no one had learned to communicate with them or was willing to live as primitively as they did. They appealed for help and I was finally able to find a dedicated Bura, a Bible student, farmer, and blacksmith named Migawa, who, with his wife and small children, was willing to go live among them and do the sacrificing necessary to build up a church in their village of Girgillang.

Migawa was a very zealous village evangelist whom I had helped train and who reported to me each Tuesday morning (market day) in Garkida. I would greet him in the laconic manner of the Buras with a "How are you with all your troubles?" as he looked a little thinner each week, and he would always reply, "Sir, where there is blessing, there is no trouble!"

This went on for some time until one day he hit me with a request I had not anticipated. "Why is it," he asked, "that I have to bring my Whona Christians to the big Garkida church to celebrate love feast where they feel completely out of place? Why can't we have the Lord's supper in Girgillang once in a while?" Well, I had never thought of such a thing and put him off a week or two. But each time he came he asked me again and I had to consider it. I discovered that there was no rule against such an arrangement and that only the inconvenience and additional planning stood in the way. I mentioned this to Migawa and he said that they would make all the necessary preparations at that end and all we would need to do would be to come!

So we set out one day and I asked for eight Bura Christians to volunteer to walk out there with me, participate in the love feast, and trudge back the same evening. It was a historic occasion. . . . I shall never forget the excitement of coming up over a rise and seeing, on a small table under a large shade tree, this gleaming white homespun tablecloth with the elements for the communion service on it! Yes, they had prepared everything, including food for the meal and barrels of water and small pans for the feetwashing.

With the advent of Brethren foreign missions in the early twentieth century, a mixed company of cultures became common at love feast. Here a white missionary washes a Nigerian man's feet. BHLA Collection.

We eighteen communicants went down through the entire service, doing the scripture readings in Bura, washing one another's feet, eating the communal meal together, and sharing the bread and cup, all of it without missing a point, with ample time for explanation and testimony—a beautiful and meaningful celebration based on Isaiah 53, John 13, and 1 Corinthians 11. While concentrating on the solemn significance of the service, we were conscious of a gathering crowd of local

people around us, punctuated by the occasional barking of a dog or braying of a donkey. Seldom have I been so caught up and moved by an observance of the feast of love. At the close of the meeting I went around and greeted the old chief, the village elders, and many local citizens, all on hand to witness this grand occasion. The chief murmured something to me in Whona that was translated as "The next time that you and your people come out and hold this service, I want to be in it and I want all my village to have a part in it!"

I was too astounded at the time to ask what he meant by that, but on the way back to Garkida I had ample time to talk it over with my Bura Christians. What they explained to me was essentially as follows: The Whona chief is an old man. He can remember when the first white men came in (the British colonial officers) and sent off his young men to work on the roads or forced them to fight in their wars. But this is the first time in his long life that he has seen a white man get down on his knees in the dark and wash a black man's feet! And if that is what this new religion (Christianity) means, he wants it and he wants all his people to have a part in it!

The old chief didn't understand a word of what was read or said in the service, but he saw all that was done and the action spoke for itself, a message he would never forget!

—*Chalmer E. Faw, McPherson, Kansas*

When meeting began, as brethren came in, I saw some of these bearded men kissing each other. These holy kisses, as will be seen hereafter, are frequent among the dunkers, and, as the men shave only the upper lip, it seems strange to us who are unaccustomed to the sight and the sound. the oft-repeated kissing was to me, perhaps, the least agreeable part of the ceremonial.

—*Phebe Gibbons,* The Plain People

Meditation

A certain baseball card, sold in a pack of ten for a nickel in the 1950s, is now worth several thousand dollars. A share of stock sold five years ago for over a hundred dollars is now virtually worthless. It is said that in Germany during the inflationary 1920s it once took a whole wheelbarrow load of Deutschmarks to buy a single loaf of bread. Today the Deutschmark is one of the strongest currencies in the world.

In this world, values often change. An economist might be able to explain, but for most of us it remains something of a mystery. Why, for example, are air fares this week only half or two thirds what they were last week? It leaves us uncertain, wondering where to turn to find some real source of enduring value.

In the church we proclaim that the source is God and that it is made known in God's word, the scriptures. Those things of eternal value are the things God values—humility, loyalty, justice, mercy, and service. Tonight through the washing of feet, we again remind ourselves of this divine economy. For obvious reasons it is a hands-on lesson in humility, loyalty, and service: We humble ourselves to perform it; our participation expresses our loyalty to the church through which the love of God has come to us; and it symbolizes the many forms of service to which our energies may be given.

But feetwashing can also be a reminder of the value of justice and

Work camp participant Joan Mangum washes the feet of Francisco Rodriguez in San Francisco, Honduras. Photo by David Radcliff.

71

mercy in the divine economy. It reminds us of justice, because it was the role of the slave to wash feet. When we remember that our Lord was willing to identify with this oppressed class of people, we realize that we too must identify with the oppressed in our own time. It reminds us of mercy, because it symbolizes the grace of our Lord that cleanses us: the forgiveness of sins. We can receive this forgiveness only if we are willing to let it flow through us when it comes to us. Remember the prayer that the Lord taught us: "Forgive us our debts, as we forgive our debtors."

I don't know what a Mickey Mantle rookie card will be worth in the year 2000. I don't know which direction the Dow Jones is headed. I don't know if you should trade dollars for Deutschmarks or Yen. But I know the values in the divine economy, and I understand why our tradition has now practiced the feetwashing for nearly three hundred years. Some values don't change.

—*James Benedict, Union Bridge, Maryland*

Few fledgling pastors have been as blessed as I with mentors. There were two African American ministers who were members of the first church I pastored, and they were there to help instruct me my first three years in the ministry. Forrest Hawkins was one. Nolan Porter was the other. Their advice and example helped complement my seminary education.

Forrest was probably in his late fifties. He had a stylish moustache and dark black hair brushed straight back. He was a small, wiry character, whose voice had more of the gravel that makes African American preaching so singular. Before leaving on a business trip, he'd stand and tell us what we meant to him, just in case he never saw us again.

One spring Forrest was preparing to fly back to Chicago to take care of some business. This was a pretty regular occurrence. Unfortunately, the timing was such that he'd miss our love feast. No matter. He called and suggested he and I get together for a private feetwashing.

I didn't check the polity manual to see if such a situation was kosher. Forrest wasn't the sort to be gainsaid. We gathered together in a little room next to the church office. We brought in basins and the bread and cup. Forrest told me what the feetwashing meant in the tradition in which he'd grown up and how he enjoyed the fact that Brethren practiced it, too. Finally we took turns bending the knee to wash the other's feet, and later shared the bread and cup as well. We parted as Christian brothers.

Soon after, at worship, he told the congregation how much we all meant to him and how he was traveling to a distant place, Chicago, and how he didn't know if he might come back. All of it was very familiar, but a few days later we received word that he'd died suddenly of a heart attack.

It was only then that I realized how much Forrest had structured the time for us to say good-bye, and I was moved that his strongest desire had been to obey the Lord through this most singular ordinance and that he wanted me to share this with him.

—*Frank Ramirez*

A wooden tub of the sort used by the Brethren to wash feet in colonial America. The tub and towel have become a symbol among Brethren of service and self-sacrificial love as well as the willingness to receive love and service. BHLA Collection.

Our first feetwashing was so important to me. It was the moment when my husband, John, and I chose to come into the Church of the Brethren. We had been attending the Kokomo Church of the Brethren and finished our membership classes by World Communion Day in October of 1965. I asked the pastor if we could attend the love feast and we did. We were originally Quakers, so this was seeing symbolism for the first time and the symbols just spelled out exactly the way we wanted to live our lives. So that's the night we became Brethren. We finished the love feast and asked to have our letters of membership transferred to the Church of the Brethren.

—Phyllis Carter, Goshen, Indiana

I grew up in a typical Brethren congregation. When we had love feast, the men and women sat at different tables and washed feet at the tables. I wasn't allowed to wash feet until I became a member. I almost always sat by my mother and had the opportunity to both wash her feet and have my feet washed by her. That was not an unusual experience since I'm sure my mother washed me during my early childhood years anyway.

After we moved to Portland, Oregon, in the early '70s, love feast was opened up a bit by having men and women sit at the same tables and go to separate areas to wash feet. By the late '70s, some people at church wanted to experiment by having men and women wash feet, an unheard of thing in most places. But Portland wasn't like most places. By 1980 we had developed a system for love feast that provided men-only and women-only tables, and the rest of us sat where we pleased and washed feet with whomever we sat by. It was a system that worked well, and there were few complaints. In fact, there was probably an increase in attendance since new members were more likely to be attracted to an inclusive style than older members.

One of my most precious memories came some time after we had changed our style. My parents were visiting during Easter week. We went to love feast as usual, and we sat together as a family. It was during the washing of feet that the moment came. I frankly don't remember whether I washed his feet or whether he washed my feet. But as my father and I exchanged the hug of fellowship, both of us had tears in our eyes. It was the first time that we had the opportunity to share this sacred ritual together. Being able to share that with my father as well as my mother was very special indeed and brings tears to my eyes even as I write this.

—Jan Eller, Portland, Oregon

Brother Sayler's favorite double mode of feet-washing, . . . you may rest assured has no higher origin than the fertile brain of the mystic Conrad Beisel.

—Abraham Harley Cassel,
in History of the Tunkers

The holy kiss? When I was growing up that was very commonly practiced. All the older people especially would greet each other, and the younger people as well. But the younger people would not always initiate it. As soon as I was baptized, the older brethren would greet me after meeting with a kiss.

In the old love feast, the kiss was used a number of times. In fact, according to earlier descriptions of Brethren love feast, one thing that impressed some of the outsiders was all the kissing that was done, which was not as normal then as it perhaps is today. All the kissing done among the Brethren was looked upon as a sort of strange thing. During love feast every time you washed and dried a brother's feet, you would both stand up and greet each other with a kiss.

The kiss was passed throughout the entire congregation. The last brother would come forward to kiss the elder who had started the circle, so there was an unbroken circle of the right hand of fellowship and the kiss of peace. At the same time, the elder would go to the sister's side and take the hand of the sister, who was usually his wife. She would kiss the sister next to her, who would then kiss the sister next to her, and so on. The unbroken circle would be completed on the sisters' side when the last sister was brought up to kiss the first sister. This was to say that every one was in unity and every one was at peace with one another and ready to take communion.

—*Clarence Kulp, Harleysville, Pennsylvania*

*Brothers extend the right hand of fellowship
and share the holy kiss after washing feet.*
Photo by William F. Smith (BHLA Collection).

Greet one another with
a holy kiss. All the churches
of Christ greet you.
(Rom. 16:16)

All the brothers and sisters
send greetings. Greet one
another with a holy kiss.
(1 Cor.16:20)

Greet one another
with a holy kiss.
(2 Cor. 13:12)

Greet all the brothers and
sisters with a holy kiss.
(1 Thess. 5:26)

Greet one another with
a kiss of love. Peace to all
of you who are in Christ.
(1 Pet. 5:14)

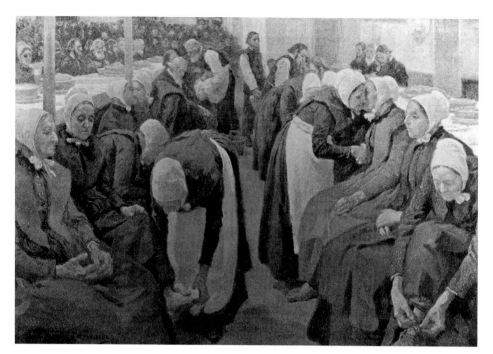

The Brethren practice of the love feast was a curiosity for outsiders. Clifford Howard rendered the ordinance of feetwashing in his painting, "A Peace Loving People," sharing the Brethren tradition with a curious nation in Ladies Home Journal, *vol. 15 (July 1898).*

Annual Meeting 1888, *Full Report*

In the emission of every breath that vibrates this mortal system of ours, there is to a certain extent a deposit lodged in the full beard that if the body is diseased, a part of it is lodged there. If there is a catarrhal affection in the head a part of it is lodged there. If there are unsound teeth or the fumes of tobacco a part of it is lodged there. Now, my dear brethren, this makes it very unpleasant to us who feel that we would like to extend to them with the heart of love the right hand of fellowship accompanied with the salutation of the holy kiss. It goes a little further than this, my dear brethren, when it comes to the communion table, those who at least would prefer a better state of things sometimes will receive the communion cup after it has been sifted through two or three or five or eight moustaches. . . . would it not be reasonable, brethren, and just that our brethren should at least go this far as to trim their moustache back to such an extent that the salutation can pass in harmony and peace and union, and thus destroy that feeling of—I do not know how to express it—that feeling which often occurs on occasions when we meet brethren with a full beard.

—*J. C. Whitmer*

We occasionally meet a brother who lets the hair in his moustache or on his lip grow down over his mouth entirely and . . . sometimes [it] is [so] saturated with tobacco juice that it looks entirely yellow. Now I appeal to this meeting if a brother is required to salute another when he finds him in that condition. . . . Brethren sometimes in the winter go out when it is cold, where the moustache is left to grow over the mouth down, and it gets naturally a little wet from the breath, and I have met brethren whose moustaches were full of ice from the top down, and they have offered me the salutation in that condition, and I made up my mind after this I would make my arm stiff.

—*Valentine Blough*

I have always been so that I could touch the lip of my brother, but I do believe, brethren, if we all wore our beards in the full image God wanted us to that half a dozen hairs in our salutation would never hinder us or come between us, because the love of God in our hearts would cover it all. And I tell you when we come to the communion cup, as it was intimated, I never think of such a thing. My mind is way back, and I remember what the Lord has done for me. I never watch who drinks out of that cup or anything about it. And hence let us never bring that in question. Let us not bring tobacco in question or rotten teeth or catarrah. . . .

—*John Forney*

After Diana, a Honduran exchange student in my school, had been in the United States for a month, I invited her to accompany my family and me to love feast at our church, the Codorus Church of the Brethren. Her English was not very good at that point and my Spanish was virtually nonexistent.

The love feast I shared with Diana was one of the most meaningful services I have ever attended. For the first time, I tried to "explain" each element of the service to someone who did not even speak my language. As the service progressed, we would try to find the relevant scripture text in her Spanish Bible so that she could follow along.

Having been raised in the Catholic Church, Diana was quite familiar with communion, but feetwashing was another matter. I still remember the wonder on her face as she looked around the room at people bending down to wash one another's feet. I still see clearly the smile on her face as I bent down to wash her feet. The reverence with which she, in turn, washed the feet of another taught me a great deal.

It has been almost twenty years since I have seen Diana, but the lessons she taught me are still fresh. Seeing love feast through her eyes opened my eyes to the beauty, the wonder, the holiness, and the importance of that service. Every action was important because it had to convey meaning to my friend who had no other way of understanding.

Diana attended love feast again the following spring when her English and my Spanish were much improved. We both appreciated sharing the service together when we could actually communicate with words. But nothing will ever replace our first, almost wordless, service of love feast and holy communion when actions spoke much louder than any words ever could.

—*Christy J. Waltersdorff, Lombard, Illinois*

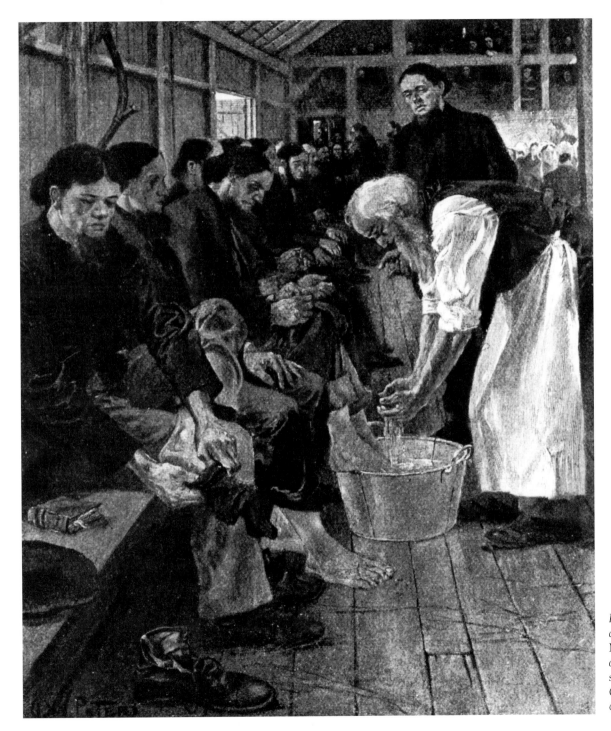

They [the Antietam Church] have a sister ninety-two years old, whose mental faculties are unimpaired. She has a traditional knowledge from old members in her early age. She never knew or heard of any other than the double mode [of feet-washing].

—*D. P. Sayler, in* History of the Tunkers

Love feast was often held in a barn to accommodate large crowds. In this illustration for an article in Scribner's Magazine (*November 1901*), *brothers used the "double mode" of feetwashing in which two men (one to wash and one to dry) serve a group of brothers until two more men take their place. Children and the curious watch from the hay loft.* Painting by G. W. Peters.

Daniel Sayler was a minister, elder, respected speaker, Annual Meeting moderator, and staunch defender of the "double mode" of feetwashing. Photo by John D. Fredency (BHLA Collection).

Note: On Whit-Monday of 1872, Annual Meeting received a report from D. P. Sayler on the matter of feetwashing.

Dear Brethren: In compliance with appointment by annual meeting of 1871, Art. 37, to ascertain, as far as possible, what was the first mode in the observance of the ordinance of feet-washing by the brethren in America, I . . . started on a tour the 27th of September, 1871, in my private conveyance, taking with me Elder Moses Miller, who kindly consented to go along. I was out 8 days, and traveled upward of 300 miles, traveling as many as 47 miles a day. . . . We also visited all the oldest members named to us, in order to ascertain all the traditional information we could.

We did not find Samuel Harley, elder of the Indian Creek church, at home, neither A. H. Cassel, they having gone to a love-feast some distance away. This I regretted much, though Brother Cassel's son kindly showed us through his father's library, but, of course, we could ascertain nothing by a personal inspection of manuscript, etc., not knowing where to find them. In order to meet this deficiency I appointed Brother Abraham H. Price, who, in my stead, should have Brother Cassel to search all the written manuscripts in his library to obtain all the written information on the subject, and write the same to me. In compliance with this arrangement Brother Price writes: "November 18, 1871. I have done as you have requested me to do. I asked Brother Cassel whether he had a journal of the ancient church that would show or tell how the German Baptists practiced feet-washing. He said he had. Yes, a journal he has from the Germantown church wherein we can see many things to our satisfaction of the housekeeping of the old brethren in the church. But nothing of feet-washing, whether single or double, nothing in his library. But he has much to tell of what he heard of old Brother Fox and others. They tell him that single mode was the practice of the mother church in Germantown."

—D. P. Sayler, in History of the Tunkers

The article from the pen of Brother Daniel P. Sayler in the *Brethren's Advocate* of March 30 was so far from the truth that I concluded it did not merit a reply, and would have held my peace, if brethren had not requested me to reply. I will, therefore, in the fear of the Lord, try to do so.

In the first paragraph he says: "In compliance with appointment by annual meeting of 1871, to ascertain as far as possible how the brethren first washed feet in America, I made as thorough an investigation of the subject as then could be made," etc. Now, let me tell, with the strictest regard to truth, how thorough that investigation was made.

He (Sayler) came here with another brother who is also an elder (but because he has so far held his peace, I will not now mention his name) [it was Elder Moses Miller] on a Saturday afternoon. I was not at home when they came, but they were kindly received by my family (who were all members), and requested to stay, as I would soon be home, but they would not. My son and others of the family pressed them to stay, as it was our regular meeting Sunday, and it so happened that we had no preacher, therefore they were the more anxious that they should stay and preach for us; but no, they would not, and stayed all night (unknown to us) near by with a stranger where they had no business. But while they were here, Brother Sayler said they would for

Abraham Harley Cassel was a self-taught man whose first language was German. He devoted a life-time to collecting books and ancient documents of the Brethren. From evidence in his extensive library, Cassel was able to show that the original mode of feetwashing among Brethren was the "single mode." Robert C. Bucher Collection.

Make no change whatever in the mode and practice of feet-washing, and stop the further agitation of the subject.

—Resolution of 1872 Annual Meeting, in History of the Tunkers

all like to see the library, so as to have an idea of its nature and size. My son then took them up (the room is forty feet long in the clear), and they walked through to the end of it on the one side, and back again on the other to the stairway, without asking a question or looking at anything, and were altogether hardly five minutes in it. They then reported that they had been to see Brother Cassel, but found nothing on feet-washing, as he asserts.

This, dear brethren, is the truth, and to corroborate it I say that in all my intercourse with the brethren I have not found a bitterer enemy to the single mode than Daniel P. Sayler. He had to come here because he was expressly ordered to see me, as I was informed. But he did not want to see me or anything pertaining to the single mode, and so he artfully slipped through, without seeing anything, in the manner just told. And what makes it still worse, the neighbor with whom they stayed overnight says that after supper he offered to walk with them up to my house, or he would bring them up, but they would not.

—Abraham Harley Cassel, in History of the Tunkers

You and I can sympathize with Peter. But our reasons for objecting to washing feet are different from Peter's. He initially refused to have his feet washed because the idea of his master doing a slave's work was repellent. We object because washing another person's feet is an outdated act. Nobody does it anymore. In our culture people wash their own feet. "I'd rather do it myself, thank you very much."

Jesus' response to Peter is instructive. He told the outspoken fisherman that unless he washed his feet Peter would have no part in him, would "have nothing in common" with him, as one translation puts it.

As self-made, self-sufficient men and women, we take umbrage at having a brother or sister do for us what we think we can do for ourselves. Jesus' words remind us that there are some things we cannot do for ourselves. We cannot earn our way into God's favor. We cannot give ourselves new life. We cannot wash our own feet.

This truth came home to me several years ago when I received a letter from an 83-year-old man living in Canada. He had read an article I had written for a church magazine and wished to share an experience he had. He described how he had fallen and broken his hip and was taken to the hospital.

I was very gloomy. Alone in a room. The night nurse came sneaking in and found me weeping. (No, I was not pitying

Power of the Towel

Walk a mile with your brother, offer to go two.
Stop to lend a helping hand, even when you're through.
Stop to think, remind yourself, He's the way, the life,
and live your life in the power of the towel.

Gird yourself, wrap the towel around your aching soul;
bind yourself with a symbol of God's love for you.
Shroud yourself in the face of this broken world and this
    darkening hour
Clothe yourself in the power of the towel.

Give today all you have, you will be repaid.
Share your love with those around, the memories won't fade.
Pause to rest and fill yourself with the bread of life
and live your life in the power of the towel.

—Jonathan A. Shively

When we attended Bethel Church of the Brethren in Northern Indiana in the 1950s, three of the twenty-three members of the congregation were physically unable to wash feet, so one year these three people began to practice the washing of one another's hands at love feast. When we moved to the Goshen City Church of the Brethren, we brought the practice of hand washing with us. Here we hold love feast on Palm Sunday morning, which enables the elderly in our congregation to attend more easily than services in the evening. When we provided a separate table with twelve seats for those who were unable to wash feet, we found that the spaces filled up quickly and people waited outside the hall for a turn. All but a very few of those in line chose this method because of their physical limitations, not because they preferred washing hands to washing feet. The congregation delighted in the presence of those who had long since stopped coming to love feast because of their physical limitations.

—*Naomi Waggy, Goshen, Indiana*

myself, but had no plans what to do next.) The following morning a nurse came into the room, supplied me with a basin of water and left me to do what I could.

Later she came to do my back and when coming to my feet said, "I believe I shall get you up into the chair and let you soak your feet while I change your bed."

When I was sitting there with my feet immersed in a deep basin of warm water, I asked, "Do you know what this reminds me of?"

"No, what?" she wondered.

So I quoted: "Supper being ended Jesus laid aside his garments and took a towel and girded himself. Afterward he poured water into a basin and began to wash the disciples' feet."

Here I paused to see whether there would be any response. After a bit of reflection she replied: "I have never thought of it that way but it surely gives a person a nice feeling to have it applied like that."

After she had completed the bed, she took another towel, folded it together and kneeled upon it in front of my feet, moistened her hands and rubbed some soap on them and tenderly washed my feet without the use of a wash cloth. Needless to say, I was deeply moved.

Moved and, I would add, blessed. As I was blessed by reading those words scrawled in a shaky hand by an old man I never met.

—*Kenneth L. Gibble,* Once Upon A Wonder

I traveled a long distance one time as a boy and forded two rivers to attend a love feast at the Pleasant Hill church. A man from way beyond there rode in on horseback. He must have heard a lot of wild stories about the love feast, so he journeyed over to see what the Brethren was up to. The Pleasant Hill church had two long tables that run the entire length of the building, one on the right-hand side for the sisters and one on the left-hand side for the brothers. In the old churches they had it that way.

This unknown man, he had a mustache. No Brethren wore a mustache. But nobody knew the stranger, and they thought he might possibly be Brethren. The house and all around outside was crowded with members and spectators. The singing started and all of the people began to go in. The stranger saw the crowd moving down, down, down. And he went right along with the crowd; he didn't know what he was getting into. They slipped in around the tables, and he did too. There he was, and either direction he'd have to walk over ten or fifteen people's feet to get out to the spectators from the row of brethren he was in.

They had the examination service. And here they come washing feet. He maybe didn't belong to any church, I don't know. But somebody washed his feet, and to keep in the tune of things he washed the next fellow's feet. They passed around the salutation: Here come a man a-kissing him, and he kissed the next man. Then they had the *agape* supper with the broth and all, and after that the communion bread and cup. I studied the visitor with lively interest and wondered what in the world he figured he had got into.

—*Reuel B. Pritchett,* On the Ground Floor of Heaven

ten / sein Kreutz auch nehmen auf / an statt der Sünden Bürden.

14. Die aber seinem Wort / noch wie-derstreben werden / die seynd noch unterm Zorn / erlangen nicht das Leben / sie bleiben in den Todt / und sterben auch in Sünden / an jenem grossen Tag/ wird GOttes Zorn anzünden.

24.

Ein Lied bey dem Fuß-waschen.
Mel. Kommt her zu mir/ spricht rc.

ACh wie so lieblich und wie fein / ist es wann Brüder einig seyn / im Glau-ben und in Liebe / wenn sie einander kön-nen recht / die Füsse waschen als treu-nen Knecht/ aus Hertzens Demuht-Triebe.

2. Diß ist köstlich und Ehrens werth/ weil selbst der HErr auff dieser Erd / die Jüngern Füß gewaschen aus Liebe / den hat gezeiget auch / wie er aus Liebe diesen Brauch / gestifft aus Demuths-Triebe.

3. Und auch dabey gesprochen hat / ich bin ein Meister in der That / wie ihr mich auch erkennet / ein Fürbild ich euch nun gemacht / aus Liebe in derselben Nacht / wie Judas sich getrennet.

4. Daß ihr solt im Gedächtniß han/ was euer Meister hat gethan / und was er euch geheissen / wie ihr einander lieben solt/ und nur sich keiner trennen wolt / wie Judas der Verrähter.

5. So last uns denn bedencken recht/in die-ser Stund als treue Knecht/was fuß-wasche bedeutet/damit wir doch in Demuht auch /
aus

Ach wie so lieblich und wie fein

O how lovely and fine it is when brethren are united in faith and love, when they can truly wash one another's feet as faithful servants out of their hearts' humble desire. (:1)

Let us then as faithful servants properly contemplate in this hour the meaning of footwashing, so that in humility we may observe this custom out of love and prepare ourselves for suffering. (:5)

For whoever will have one's feet washed must remember how the Lord did this and what an important part of it is in the cleansing of the soul and the sanctification, washed by the Lord (:7)

For whoever refuses to be washed by the Lord and his congregation [*Gemeine*] has no part in her life and will remain in his or her own ways and the soul will remain a withered vine in all eternity. (:8)

[All this is order] that we may continue to proclaim your death and your great anguish [*Angst*], and in so doing break your bread and learn what it means to have communion [*Gemeinschaft*] with your true life. (:10)

—*Attributed to William Knepper,* Geistreiches Gesang-Buch, *Berleburg, Germany, 1720. These five verses are translated by Hedwig T. Durnbaugh in* The German Hymnody of the Brethren *1720-1903.*

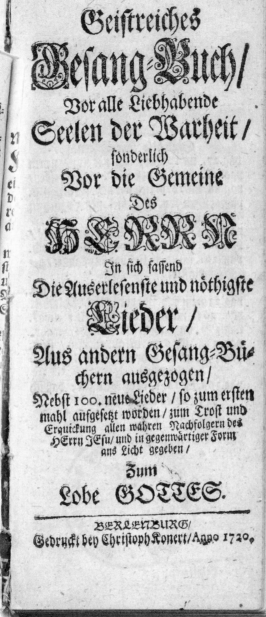

(44)

aus Lieb begehen diesen Brauch / uns schi-
cken zu dem Leiden.

6. Und auch zu wahrer Einigkeit / einander lieben ohne Neid / in Demuht recht von
Hertzen / ach daß kein Judas sey dabey /
der dieses thu aus Heucheley / welches der
Seele macht Schmertzen.

7. Dann wer sein Fuß will waschen
lahn / muß mercken wies der HErr gethan / und muß dabey gedencken / wie
nöhtig sey die Reinigung / der Seelen
und die Heiligung / gewaschen von dem
Herren.

8. Denn wer nicht will gewaschen
seyn / vom Herrn und seiner Gemein / der
hat kein Theil im Leben / wird bleiben in
der Eigenheit / und seine Seel in Ewigkeit /
wird seyn ein dürrer Reben.

9. Nun denn Herr Jesu mach uns
gleich / zu grünen Reben in deinem Reich /
und auch in deiner Gemeine / erfülle uns
mit Fried und Lieb / durch deines wahren Geistes Trieb / dir folgen gantz
alleine.

10. Daß wir auch ferner deinen Todt /
wie auch dein grosse Angst und Noht /
verkündigen gar eben / und dein Brodt
brechen auch dabey / erkennen was Ge-
meinschafft sey / mit deinen wahren Leben.

11. Nun denn HErr Jesu zum Be-
schluß / schenck dazu deines Geistes Guß /
jetzund kräfftig von oben / so wollen wir
in dieser Stund / aus unserm gantzen
Hertzens-Grund / dein grosse Lieb nach-
leben.

26. Mel.

Geistreiches
Gesang-Buch /
Vor alle Liebhabende
Seelen der Warheit /
sonderlich
Vor die Gemeine
Des
HERRN
In sich fassend
Die Auserlesenste und nöthigste
Lieder /
Aus andern Gesang-Bü-
chern ausgezogen /
Nebst 100. neue Lieder / so zum ersten
mahl aufgesetzt worden / zum Trost und
Erquickung allen wahren Nachfolgern des
HErrn JEsu / und in gegenwärtiger Form
ans Licht gegeben /
Zum
Lobe GOTTES.

BERLENBURG /
Gedruckt bey Christoph Konert / Anno 1720.

*From the beginning Brethren worshiped with singing. Of the hymns collected in the
first Brethren hymnal (1720), one hundred were new hymns, many of them written by
Brethren. Hymn 24 makes reference to feetwashing and is attributed to Wilhelm Knepper, one of the Solingen Brethren imprisoned in Germany for their religious beliefs.*

My name is Isaac Clarence Kulp. I was born in the house I still live in, in the village of Verfield, just outside of Harleysville, Pennsylvania. I was baptized in the west branch of the Percium Creek nearby in the late 1940s in the month of January. There was no ice on the creek but the water was cold. When my mother was baptized in Indian Creek in 1914, they had to break several inches of ice.

We always went to love feast at the Indian Creek Church of the Brethren meeting house when I was growing up until about 1953 when they remodeled the meetinghouse and protestantized it. Before that, all the brethren sat on one side and the sisters sat on the other side. We had the old type of Dunkard love feast benches. The back was hinged to the end, and you could turn it up and make it into a table, so when we had love feast, the meeting room was filled with tables with benches on either side and you faced each other on either side. There was a long preacher's table, filled at love feast time with visiting preachers from neighbor congregations. The table seated at least a dozen to fifteen Brethren, depending on how tight they sat—a very long table. I remember that one of my first impressions was seeing all of these bearded faces in a row behind the table.

When we were children we would go with our parents to love feast. And in those days, whether you were a boy or a girl, you'd go with your mother and sit on the sisters' side. At first we were held by our mother, and then later we'd sit on the bench alongside of her; then there came a certain age, as I remember maybe about five or six years old, when both boys and girls would sit on the men's side. As we got a little bit older than that, we'd sit with the boys or girls on boys or girls benches by ourselves with no adult supervision. Each time was sort of like a graduation. It felt real good to be deemed old enough to sit by yourself.

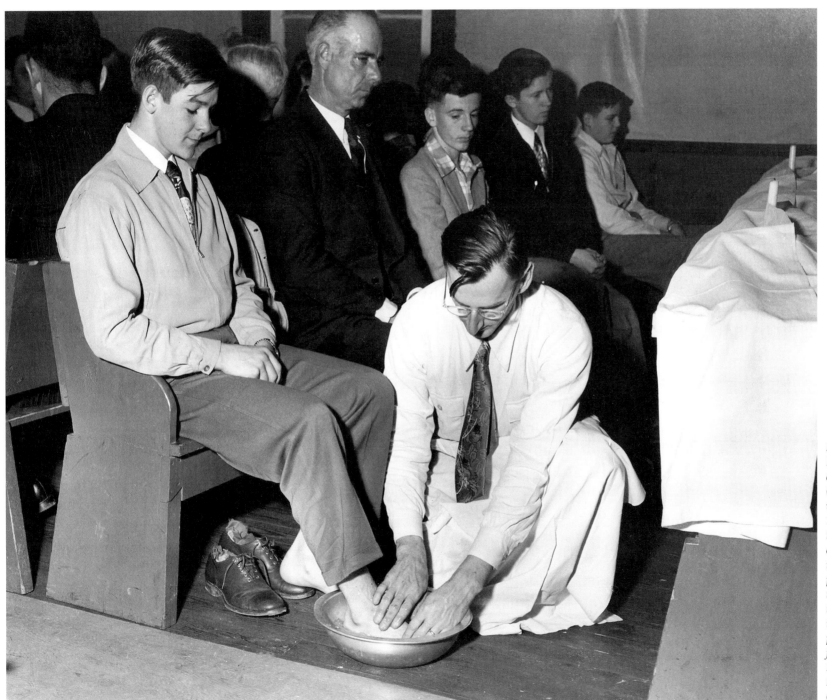

Men of the Evergreen congregation (Virginia) wash feet in 1951. The table in front of them is made from a pew. The food is covered by the tablecloth until participants finish feetwashing.
Photo by J. Henry Long (BHLA Collection).

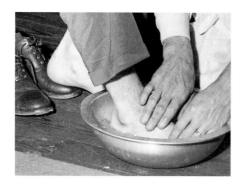

I would further say that since his visit here I traveled through Maryland, and stayed with Brother Sayler all night, and to his credit I say, he received me very kindly as a brother in the Lord. It was a cold, chilly October evening, so after supper he raked up the fire and said, "Now, Brother Cassel, sit here by me, and let us have a real old-fashioned talk." "What shall be the subject, Brother Daniel?" said I. "Oh, anything at all," he replied, "except feet-washing! I will hear nothing about that, for you have your views and I have mine, and I mean to hold to what I have. Therefore, there is no use talking about it." And so my visit to him passed off without saying anything more about it. For, from his previous knowledge of me, he knew very well that I had such overwhelming testimonies in favor of the single mode that he could not overcome them, and therefore he would not hear or see anything relating to it.

—*Abraham Harley Cassel, in* History of the Tunkers

I remember when I was a little older I found several older Brethren, particularly one, that I liked very much, and I would go and sit with one of these older Brethren in the section where the old men sat. I also remember when I was still pretty young, I pestered my parents to buy me a hat so I could hang my hat on the suspended hat rack next to this old brother's hat. I could not actually reach the hat rack. He'd reach and get it for me.

In some areas they would go from the tables to a special area to wash feet, but we always washed feet at the table. Someone would begin washing at one end and he would wash the man next to him, and on around the table, and the last one would wash the one who started. All tables washed simultaneously.

I remember also at love feast that when we were children we would sit with one of our parents when the elders distributed the bread. The loaves of unleavened bread were broken into long strips; then the elders would come down the aisle and hand the strips into the row and each brother would break a piece and give it to the next brother, and so on. Each one would say "Dear brother, this bread which we break is the communion of the body of Christ" as he handed the strip to the next brother. When the strip was down to only one piece left, not large enough to break, it would be given to the elder, who would lay it on the edge of his tray and hand in another long strip to be broken. After the brethren and sisters had been served, he'd take the end pieces and give them to the children in attendance who had not been baptized. This was not deemed an official act because the communion bread had not been broken for the child and the words were not spoken over it. I remember when I received one of these end pieces I would lay it on the table next to my father's piece of bread, and it made me feel a part of the ritual.

In our particular tradition in this part of Pennsylvania, the love feast meal was sliced beef on platters, plates of bread and butter, and bowls of the beef broth. Now in Lancaster County, they would put rice and broken bread in the broth, but as far as I know, we never did that in Montgomery County.

The first settler in Indian Creek was John Jacob Price in 1719, followed by the Harleys, the Stauffers, and several other early families. As far as I've been able to determine, our love feast came to us from the original congregation in Germantown. Ours was the original method of conducting the love feast.

In the late eighteenth century, Germantown and Chester County changed the love feast and began serving cheese and sweet rolls and coffee, which was quite different. In fact, there was a preacher, I believe it was David Sauer (Christopher Sauer's son), who wrote a letter of complaint about the change in the love feast because he could no longer get a good hearty piece of beef and broth, but cheese.

Here in our congregation we used the common cup until some time in the 1950s, when we got the individual cups. That, the children didn't get. The elders would pass the cup from the end of the bench, from brother to brother. During the cup we sang hymns, usually about the blood of Christ.

In my grandparents' time, love feast was only once a year, in the spring. During my parents time that changed, and it was usually held in May and October. Our congregation now has it on Maundy Thursday and World Communion Sunday, but that was a very recent change. In any given area, the neighboring congregations would try not to have it on the same weekends. For example, if there were four Brethren congregations, they might have it on the four Sundays in May with each one having it on a different Sunday. That was so everyone could visit the other love feasts.

—*Clarence Kulp, Harleysville, Pennsylvania*

Suppose that Jesus Christ had laid down the abstract doctrine—Christians, ye ought to wash one another's feet. What would have been the result? Who would have believed him? We should have found in that an instance of mistranslation; there would have been great hunting up of grammars and lexicons upon that point, because it stands to reason that the thing is utterly absurd. There is a missing letter; there is a wrong punctuation; there is a great difference of opinion between critics, we should have said, as to the meaning of this. But what does Jesus Christ do? Instead of merely laying down the doctrine, he gave the example. . . . There it was,—a stoop that could never be forgotten, an argument which no ingenuity could ever impair. It was worth doing, or he who never trifled with life would not have set us the example.

—*Joseph Park, in* An Exegetical Study of the Events Immediately
  Preceding the Farewell Messages of Our Lord

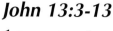

John 13:3-13

1 Jesus rises from the table and lays aside (*tiqhsi*) his outer garments (*ta imatia*) (v. 4).

2 Jesus takes a towel and wraps it about himself (*diexwsen eauton*), puts water in a basin and begins to wash his disciples' feet (a menial task often assigned to slaves; 1 Sam. 25:41; cf Mark 1:7; Acts 13:25) (v.5).

3 When Jesus finishes he once again takes his outer garments and puts them on (*elaben ta imatia*), and again sits down at the table (*anepesen*) from which he got up (v. 12).

4 Finally Jesus says: "you should address me as teacher and Lord (*Kurios*) and you are right, for that is what I am" (v. 13).

Philippians 2:6-11

1 He emptied himself (*ekenwsen eauton*). Moffatt translates: "He laid it [his divine nature] aside" (v. 7).

2 . . . taking the form of a slave, being born in the likeness of human beings. And being found in human form he humbled himself (*etapeinwsen eauton*) (v. 8).

3 Therefore God also highly exalted him to the highest place and gave him the name that is above every name (v. 9).

4 . . . that every tongue might openly confess that Jesus Christ is Lord (*kurios*, v. 11).

—*Gerald F. Hawthorne,* Philippians

AGAPE MEAL

Aunt Magdalene Sherfy was a great church worker, a sister to my mother's mother and a famous midwife. Her husband was dead, and she had lost six or seven children in a row with scarlatina, though two girls lived through. She always said there was a peculiar aroma, a sacred aroma, a well-pleasing aroma that went up from the beef at Love Feast into the nostrils of the Lord. And she proved it by two places in the old Bible about God smelling the sacrifices. Well, the best soup I ever did eat I've eaten at the Love Feast—and I've tasted some that wasn't so good. But those old sisters back in my boyhood days, they knew how to make it.

—*Reuel Pritchett*

Agape Meal

IN 1998 Brother Norman Harsh surveyed congregations on the love feast. The survey shows that most Churches of the Brethren refer to the re-enactment of the last supper as "love feast" or "love feast and communion." They eat a full meal and have bread and cup communion besides. Most Christians call this event the Lord's Supper, referring just to communion. Why then do Brethren have both a full meal and the bread and cup?

Scripture calls for two kinds of meals. The last supper tradition is based on Matthew 26:17-29; Mark 14:12-16; and Luke 22:7-13, the stories of Jesus' last meal with the disciples in which he institutes a way for them to remember him. This is the tradition that remains today as bread and cup communion. But scripture also ordains that the community share meals together as an act of fellowship and unity. These meals are called *agape* meals, a Greek term whose earliest use in the Bible is found in Jude 12 and refers not to the Eucharist but to religious feasts of the early Christians. These meals were at the heart of early Christian fellowship and worship.

While we often associate the love feast at Easter time with the Passover meal of Judaism, Graydon Snyder notes that every picture, every drawing, every sculpture of the agape meal in ancient Christian art has fish and bread and wine, the elements present in the stories of the feeding of the multitudes. There is no example, absolutely none, of a lamb. "That is to say," according to Snyder, "the Jewish Passover is gone in Christian tradition and thinking."

In the ancient church, the agape *meal was a fellowship meal based on the biblical story of the feeding of the multitudes. Ancient art depicting the agape meal usually contains the bread and fish that Jesus' disciples served to the crowds on the hillside.* Graydon Snyder Collection.

Jesus had said, in the context of the Last Supper, that he was among them, not as one who reclined at the table, but as one who serves (Luke 22:27)— essentially as one who does women's work. . . .

Ironically, during the history of the church, one of the last places women have been allowed to serve is at the Lord's table.

—*Reta Halteman Finger, in* The Lord's Supper: Believers Church Perspectives

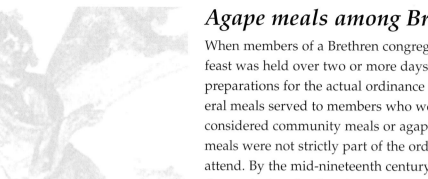

Agape meals among Brethren

When members of a Brethren congregation lived far from one another, love feast was held over two or more days to allow people to travel and make preparations for the actual ordinance of love feast and communion. The several meals served to members who were preparing for the service were also considered community meals or agape meals, but since these preparatory meals were not strictly part of the ordinance, outsiders were permitted to attend. By the mid-nineteenth century, so many spectators wanted to join in the meals that the church community was no longer able to feed everyone.

While spectators were fascinated by the novelty of it all, Brethren have always sought to be as unoriginal as possible when it comes to love feast, modeling their practice on scripture and the early church. However, Brethren are unique in one regard. It is possible that the church kitchen, now a fixture in churches of all denominations, had its origins in the Brethren love feast. Although the first Brethren met in homes and barns, it became necessary to build meetinghouses when congregations became large. The first meetinghouses resembled houses and, like houses, included kitchens so that members could prepare the most important meal of the year, the Lord's Supper. The oldest church kitchen in America might well be that located at the Pricetown Church of the Brethren in Pennsylvania.

There was a time when the agape meal was more uniform than it is now. Everyone drank out of the same dipper, and everyone ate beef. Nowadays people prefer to drink from individual cups. Then most congregations served the same food, usually beef or lamb. Now congregations take vegetarian brothers and sisters into account when preparing the meal. These options make it possible for more of God's people to eat together.

In the end the menu isn't as important as the people. There was a church whose membership was dwindling. Many of the original deacons had retired and moved away. Rather than worry about all the details of preparation, they sent someone out for food from a fast food restaurant and held their feetwashing and love feast anyway. It turned out the food wasn't as important as the main ingredient—love.

But food in general is very important. Food is more than an aid to fellowship. It *is* fellowship. Everyone has to eat. Peoples from all cultures have

Women of the ancient church served as deaconesses and took an active role in feasts. This ancient fresco depicts two women. Irene is asked to pass the hot food and Agape is asked to mix the wine and water. Graydon Snyder Collection.

Instead of believers pulling themselves together to be worthy to appear at the Lord's table, may it not be that the Lord's table graces them to live worthy of their calling?

—*Marlin Jeschke, in* The Lord's Supper: Believers Church Perspectives

recognized that we have this in common, and sharing a meal together makes us one. Moreover, eating one another's food is a way of showing acceptance, whether it's sop (the traditional meat, bread, and broth), collard greens, menudo, or kim chee.

There are other options for guests at the meal besides different foods. Most observe quiet conversation or silence during the meal, but others join in open conversation. No one knows exactly where the notion came from that people must eat in quiet. Probably not from our Jewish cousins. The Passover is not a silent celebration. Nor is it our regular practice to be silent at any other meal. Far from it. A potluck is a joyful gathering, and you can hear yourself over the din if you shout.

Some congregations eat in dim light. Others eat in full light. Some family members sit together during the meal; in other congregations, family members scatter, knowing they are part of the greater church family. Some use ceramic dinnerware and consider the clinking of china and utensils in a quiet room to be part of the atmosphere. Others use disposable plates. These differences only point up the importance of the meal and the insignificance of the details.

An odd practice in some congregations is to eat little or nothing of the food that is offered. Then after love feast, leftovers are parceled out and taken home. Taking Paul's warning to Corinthian Christians to eat at home rather than profane the table (1 Cor. 11:33), they interpret this to mean we should fill up at home and then just eat a smidge for form's sake. Paul's admonition was more likely to be directed at rich Christians who were filling up on the love feast before the poorer Christians got off work and could eat with them. Brethren today are coming to the table at the same time and are not in danger of slighting someone.

Though Corinthian Christians failed in it, the biblical ideal is to share a full meal, a hearty meal. The beloved Elder John Kline once upbraided a friend who . . .

> still insists that the breaking of bread, or the eating of a morsel of bread (sometimes merely a wafer) and a sip of wine, is the Lord's Supper. . . . Not only Scripture but reason and common sense refutes the idea; it is perverting language from its most simple and obvious

sense, and opens the way for almost any error or abuse. Supper is a
meal to satisfy the wants of nature, feast is a meal of plenty and
should the Lord's feast of charity be less? (Harry Anthony Brunk,
Brethren Life and Thought, Summer 1964, 28-29)

This is the Lord's table. All should be welcome to it and all should have
enough. If Jesus could suffer Judas, his betrayer, to eat with him, then we
should feel honored that fellow sinners seek to sit with us at God's table
as well. *F.R.*

Jeanine Wine

When they had gone ashore, they saw a charcoal fire there, with fish
on it, and bread. Jesus said to them, "Bring some of the fish that you
have just caught." So Simon Peter went aboard and hauled the net
ashore, full of large fish, a hundred fifty-three of them; and though
there were so many, the net was not torn. Jesus said to them, "Come
and have breakfast." Now none of the disciples dared to ask him,
"Who are you?" because they knew it was the Lord. Jesus came and
took the bread and gave it to them, and did the same with the fish.
This was now the third time that Jesus appeared to the disciples after
he was raised from the dead.

—*John 21:9-14*

After this Jesus went to the other side of the Sea of Galilee, also called the Sea of Tiberias. A large crowd kept following him, because they saw the signs that he was doing for the sick. Jesus went up the mountain and sat down there with his disciples. Now the Passover, the festival of the Jews, was near. When he looked up and saw a large crowd coming toward him, Jesus said to Philip, "Where are we to buy bread for these people to eat?" He said this to test him, for he himself knew what he was going to do. Philip answered him, "Six months' wages would not buy enough bread for each of them to get a little." One of his disciples, Andrew, Simon Peter's brother, said to him, "There is a boy here who has five barley loaves and two fish. But what are they among so many people?" Jesus said, "Make the people sit down." Now there was a great deal of grass in the place; so they sat down, about five thousand in all. Then Jesus took the loaves, and when he had given thanks, he distributed them to those who were seated; so also the fish, as much as they wanted. When they were satisfied, he told his disciples, "Gather up the fragments left over, so that nothing may be lost." So they gathered them up, and from the fragments of the five barley loaves, left by those who had eaten, they filled twelve baskets. When the people saw the sign that he had done, they began to say, "This is indeed the prophet who is to come into the world."

—John 6:1-14

Feed Us with Light

He went up on the mountain, mountain, mountain
he went up on the mountain and sat down there
a great many people, people, people
a great many people followed after him

They brought the lame, they brought the blind
they brought the deaf and they laid them at his feet
and he did heal them, he did heal them
and all the people were glorifying God

He told his disciples, I'm sorry for the people
with me so long and they've had nothing to eat
it's been one, it's been two,
it's been three days with nothing to eat

And I would not leave them hungry, send them home hungry
let them go hungry lest they faint upon the way.
But his disciples asked him, where in this wilderness
would we find food for such a multitude?

O then he asked them, how many loaves have you?
They said, seven and a few little fish.
He told the people, people, people
he told the people to sit upon the ground

He took the loaves, he took the fishes
he broke them and he blessed them
and he gave to his disciples to give to the people
all did eat and all were filled

All did eat and all were filled
and the food that was left filled seven baskets full

> Feed us with light, feed us with mercy
> feed us with truth, feed us with grace
> feed us with hope, feed us with loving
> feed us with joy, feed us with peace

—*Steve Kinzie*

This building was obviously designed as a place for eating meals in, for a gutter has been found close to the benches and the drain leading off from it contained fragments of glass, chicken and fish bones, ashes and sand.

—F. van der Meer, Augustine, the Bishop

A place for eating meals and a gutter containing glass fragments, fish bones, and ashes provide evidence that fellowship meals and refrigeraria, *remembrances of the dead, were held in St. Sebastian's church in Rome as early as the third century.* Graydon Snyder Collection.

St. Sebastian is built over a pagan burial site that made use of an old quarry. In the third century, it became a Christian cemetery and basilica. Graffiti commemorating lives of Christians adorns a wall below the present-day structure. Graydon Snyder Collection.

All who believed were together and had all things in common; they would sell their possessions and goods and distribute the proceeds to all, as any had need. Day by day, as they spent much time together in the temple, they broke bread at home and ate their food with glad and generous hearts, praising God and having the goodwill of all the people. And day by day the Lord added to their number those who were being saved.

—Acts 2:44-47

It was in 1975 as Mary and I were teaching at the Theological College of Northern Nigeria, an institution for training ministers and evangelists from about thirty diverse tribes and nine different denominations, that it came time for the Church of the Brethren to lead the monthly Holy Communion services. . . .

The feetwashing was new to everyone except the Brethren students, but soon caught on and was meaningful. It was, however, the communal meal that was the most noteworthy. Since, in Nigeria, we always had the communicants bring their own food, there were students with pounded yams, some with rice, some with millet, and our own Brethren with guinea corn mush and greens, to say nothing of

American and European foods! Then, Nigerian style, everyone felt that he or she should share with every other tribal group. So they got up out of their seats and began cruising around through the room, joyously dipping out food for each other, almost bedlam but so beautifully Christian that no one felt like stopping them! To be honest, this almost stole the show, and I had a hard time getting the group to quiet down and celebrate the bread and the cup in the deep, spiritual manner that we wanted.

It was a love feast such as I had never experienced before or since. And many were the thankful comments I received from non-Brethren Nigerians as to how wonderful it was the way tribes intermingled and shared, a symbol of peace and unity they would never forget.

—Chalmer E. Faw, McPherson, Kansas

A meal is an agape meal whenever there is Christian fellowship and whenever the faithful eat together and are satisfied. Nigerian Brethren feed a multitude of hungry children in true agape style. BHLA Collection.

The original building [the Germantown meetinghouse, 1770] had three levels: a basement, a street-level worship room, and an attic loft to accommodate overnight guests coming to Love Feast. A kitchen for the preparation of this semi-annual congregational fellowship meal and Communion was considered a Brethren meetinghouse essential from the first.

—Nancy Kettering Frye, "The Meetinghouse Connection: Plain Living in the Gilded Age," Pennsylvania Folklife, Winter 1991/92

Food for hundreds of love feast participants was made on this once modern wood stove and oven in a Brethren meetinghouse. The water line was a later addition. BHLA Collection.

Sop

The day before love feast, order 20 lbs boneless chuck roasts, cut in two pound pieces.

Morning of communion: Tables and chairs are set up. The communion bread is made. The table settings are set out. Three or four slices of white bread are broken up in each white enamel communion bowl (1 lid and 1 bowl per table). Lid is placed on bowl and set aside until the evening.

Cooking of meat: Use some hot water to clean the kettle.

2:00 p.m.: put two buckets of cold water in kettle. Put on the lid. Turn up the heat and leave it this way until you see steam coming out around the lid. Add meat and continue to boil.

2:30 p.m. (approximately): Turn down the heat and let the meat simmer. (Be sure heat is high enough to have some steam always coming out around the lid.)

4:30 p.m.: Check meat; continue cooking on low heat until 5:30 p.m.

5:30 p.m.: Add ½ bucket of water, 1/3 cup salt, 1 tsp pepper. Turn up the heat until the broth boils again and then turn down to simmer.

6:45 p.m.: Take up meat into two stainless steel pans from the kitchen. Put the broth in two aluminum buckets from the kitchen. Turn off both gas valves. Ladies put small pieces of beef on top of the broken bread in the bowls and then put ½ dipper of broth in each bowl. Put on the lid, and they are ready for the tables. Just wipe the big kettle with paper towel, leaving a little grease so it doesn't rust. Leave lid off until cool.

7:00 p.m.: Ready to serve.

—*Elkhart Valley (Indiana) Church of the Brethren*

Sop

30 lbs beef chuck, cut in chunks
1 lb suet

Rinse meat with water and drain. Place meat and suet in 3 gallon cooking pots, half in each, and fill with water to within 2½ inches of the top. Bring to a rolling boil, then reduce heat to a simmer. Skim off the top until broth totally clear. Add 3 tbs salt, a dash of black pepper, 3 tsp sugar, and 9-10 (or more) bouillon cubes to each cooker. Allow at least four hours for cooking until tender.

Remove meat from broth, keeping broth hot on stove. Separate meat and remove all visible fat and gristle. Replace meat into broth.

Break five pieces white fresh bread into 38 serving bowls and ladle soup into bowls right before serving. Place two slices of bread (cut in half) on plates which top each bowl. Place two bowls at each table of eight. Serves 150.

—*New Paris (Indiana) Church of the Brethren*

Missionaries have carried the Brethren love feast to the far corners of the world. Sitting on the floor, Indian Brethren prepare food for love feast. BHLA Collection.

All through my life I've heard people talk about how there is no aroma so savory and delicious as what comes up off of the beef that is cooked for the Love Feast meal. We would be sitting there around the table observing the Lord's Supper with a crowded house of spectators, standing jammed right up till there was hardly room to have the service, and them under the pressure of that beef aroma. It tantalized them; they were longing to have a sandwich or just a taste of it. When the service was over, those old deacons and deaconesses would make sandwiches and hand them toward the spectators, four or five people grabbing at the same sandwich.

—*Reuel Pritchett,* On the Ground Floor of Heaven

First Church of the Brethren, Chicago, threw a New Year's party to welcome 1971. It was a communion supper. Everyone had a great time—children, youth, adults—all agreed it was a fun evening.

Why so joyful? It's hard to say. The men agreed to fix the meal and serve it, so the ladies were more relaxed than usual. And the menu was a special "black meal"—chitterlings, spaghetti, slaw, cornbread with cracklings, and sweet potato cobbler. It was the first time "soul" food had dominated at the First Church dinner—and some of us were vaguely aware this might be the first "soul" communion in the history of the Church of the Brethren. In any case, black members enjoyed the discomfiture of soul brothers with white faces trying to down chitterlings overly smothered with Louisiana hot sauce.

Yes, there was joy there. It was the joy of the Lord. To be sure, we were in the middle of a grim, inner-city ghetto. It was Chicago—seven black youths were on trial for killing a white gang detective; a highly qualified black educator had just been blocked by white officialdom from a job as president of the board of education.

But here we were—black and white, young and old, administrators and workers, teachers and students—made one at the table of the Lord. We sang "soul" music to prepare ourselves. We saluted each other with grape [drink], speaking of the cup as the heartbeat of the new covenant in Jesus Christ. We broke fresh, warm cornbread with cracklings and spoke of the breaking of bread together as the sharing in the promised body of Christ. Then we had the Agape. For many it was just a good "down home" meal, but for others of us it was a new world. We were taking seriously Paul's comment in 1 Corinthians 11 about eating each other's food as the sign of participation in the body. As cautious whites downed the chitterlings and cornbread, blacks smiled and welcomed

The deacon women made communion bread by kneading and working the dough for hours, while the men cooked the meat. By six o'clock the aroma of the beef and bread filled the church. We may cook beef using the same recipe and method at home, but it will never smell or taste like that spread at the Lord's Supper.

—*Pearl Aldrich, North Liberty, Indiana*

us as "soul brothers" (or was the word Brethren?). . . .

At this love feast whites no longer "served" blacks but were served by blacks who brought them into their life-style. So we ended the meal by serving and being served: emphasizing the point of John 13 that one cannot take part in Jesus unless he is willing to receive life from others. . . .

Not every communion has been like this for me. Being a birthright Dunker, some of the more somber love feasts have been the high point of my Christian experience. The memories of Christ's presence at the table are sharp. I have seen fathers weep as their sons washed their feet at the "first" communion. I have seen the shabbily dressed, the mentally ill, the physically handicapped sit at the table as equal brothers and sisters. I have washed feet with black, brown, and yellow all at the same table in the same service. I have become convinced the Eucharist is the heart of the Christian faith. This is where belief and action meet. This is where the mundane converts to holy; the broken to whole; the sick to healthy. . . .

The church needs an action which articulates the action of God in Jesus Christ, defines Christianity, and includes all men who would be created in new communion (*koinonia*; 1 Cor. 10:16). I am convinced such an action would be the "full communion," which I have known from my heritage. The Swiss Protestant Jean-Jacques von Allmen, in his book *The Lord's Supper*, says the time has come for the church to restore the Agape as the means of assimilating the gospel of Jesus Christ. I would agree with him on the importance of our eating together. As some early martyrs said, "*Sine Domenico non Possumus*" (Without the Lord's meal we are powerless). At First Church we can say, "At the Lord's table we found 'soul.' "

—*Graydon F. Snyder, "Chitterling Communion: Breaking Cracklin' Cornbread Together,"*
Messenger, April 1, 1971

This long table was used often at Heidelberg (Pennsylvania) love feasts. Piled with old tin soup dishes used for the agape meal, it is pictured here in the attic of the meetinghouse. BHLA Collection.

Query to Annual Meeting 1895, *Full Report*

The Neosho County church asks the Southeastern District of Kansas to ask Annual Meeting to give a decision on the right or wrong of the church changing, on Communion occasions, our time-honored custom of dipping in the dish, and substituting a saucer for each individual member.

Responses:

. . . we all know it is a simpler thing to eat from a common dish than to dip from that dish into another one, and then eat from that. . . . Now they come up and want to argue in favor of intricacy, and I say, Let us stick to simplicity; that principle is always safe and always sure."

. . . I will simply say, Don't let us get too nice and depart from old practices. If you were to go down into the East, into the eastern country, you would find that people are not quite so delicate; they even use their fingers, and I think it is well enough.

. . . when spoons were invented, that was an innovation, and it certainly was wrong, if innovations were wrong. Just at what year did that wrong become right, and if it is wrong now to add another vessel [a saucer] between the first vessel [the common bowl] and the second vessel [the spoon], may it not be that after a while that wrong may become right? . . . We want to be governed by principle, and not by these things which have no weight in them. That is the trouble the Savior had with the Pharisees.

Answer:
We counsel our brethren to make no change in our time-honored custom in this respect.

NOTE: Since Standing Committee previously ruled that the use of saucers was wrong, this rejection of its decision is tacit permission to use individual saucers. In fact, the moderator's final comment on the matter was that the decision "doesn't say it is wrong."

Some hold [the Lord's Supper] in the morning, others, at noon, but none have it as a supper. When an evening or a noon meal is to be held, there must be something to eat! But here the people go to their so-called "supper" and return from it hungry and thirsty. Some do not even receive a bit of bread and a little wine, but at the same time are filled with great extravagance of clothes, sensual debauchery, selfish pride, and the like.

—The Complete Writings of Alexander Mack

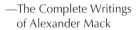

At Pricetown, on an eminence near the fork of the road, leading to the ruins of the Oley Furnace, stands the old stone church of the German Baptist denomination, popularly known as Dunkers. This is said to be the oldest building of the kind in the United States. It was erected in 1777. In its architecture it has not been changed a particle since, though its walls show the wear of the elements. . . .

It is a plain 30 x 25 one-story building with a 16 x 16 addition, both parts being constructed of rough stone. The walls are nearly two feet thick and have outworn several shingle roofs. In the early part of the last century, love feasts were held in this building regularly.

The cooking was done in the addition for which purpose it was erected, and the sisters then brought the food into the main building where the feast was held. In those days, a culinary department was distinctly necessary here. People from all over the country and from many beyond its borders attended these feasts. There was no other Dunker Church then within a radius of 40 miles, and with the exception of the Wertz and Spies churches there were no other houses of worship for a great distance. Services held in the old Dunker church were always well attended, no matter how bad the weather.

—History of the Church of the Brethren in the Eastern District of Pennsylvania, 1708-1915

The Pricetown meetinghouse, built in 1777, is the oldest unaltered Brethren meetinghouse. The small room built on the end houses the kitchen. Because of love feast preparation, Brethren meetinghouses are thought to be the first to have church kitchens. BHLA Collection.

Four men eat from one bowl at love feast in Howard Pyle's illustration for Harper's Weekly *(March 17, 1883). In 1895 Annual Meeting entertained a query as to whether Brethren should share bowls or eat from individual bowls. Eventually individual bowls replaced the common bowl.* Drawing by Howard Pyle.

On that day, December 25, 1723, three events transpired that made the first day of the mother church so memorable. In the forenoon the church was fully organized by choosing Peter Becker as their elder; in the afternoon, six applicants were baptized in the historic Wissahickon, the "first fruits" of the church in America; and, in the evening, at the home of Brother John Gommere, on the shores of the Wissahickon, near the place of baptism, the first love feast and communion service was held.

—*G. N. Falkenstein,* Two Centuries of the Church of the Brethren: Bicentennial Addresses, *1909*

Prayer

In Luke 22:14-15 we read: "When the hour came, [Jesus] took his place at table, and the apostles with him. He said to them, 'I have eagerly desired to eat this Passover with you. . . .' "

O, my brothers and sisters, I long to eat the Lord's Supper with you. I earnestly desire for us to share together in the presence of the living Christ, this event—these sacraments instituted and ordained by Him. I covet for us the simplicity, the quiet reverence, the awe, the holiness, the understandable mystery of the Lord's Supper.

—*Pearl Aldrich, North Liberty, Indiana*

Prior to the building of Elkhart Valley, the love feasts were held in barns, or out of doors. After the Elkhart Valley church house was built, it was held on the sanctuary floor. This meant the benches had to be rearranged and tables provided. Tables that had folding legs were made especially for communion. Originally the tables were stored in a near-by barn. In 1917 the tables were stored in the north end communion kitchen. Then in 1932 they were stored on the Michigan ledge in the basement. These tables were used until 1957 when new tables were purchased that are presently in use.

The old tables were constructed of prime 1″ by 12″ tulip poplar boards. They were 12′ long and 24″ wide. The legs folded toward the middle of the tables; when they were extended, a 1″ x 12″ board fell into place. Cleats on each end of the board prevented the legs from collapsing while in use. (One of the boards from these tables is known to still be in existence.)

When communion was held, teams of men removed the unneeded benches from the sanctuary. They were stored in the west side of the back kitchen. The remainder of the benches were positioned parallel to the length of the sanctuary; in between them were placed the folding tables. They were stored in the basement and when needed slid out a basement window to men outside the church who in turn slid them through a sanctuary window to men inside. After communion the order

Women in prayer coverings at First Church (Chicago) eat the agape *meal together.* Photo by F. Wayne Lawson (BHLA Collection).

Lamb Stew

Mix together ½ cup flour, 3 tsp salt, and ½ tsp pepper.

Then debone and cut 3 lbs lean shoulder of lamb into 2-inch cubes. Dredge meat in the flour mix and brown in 1/4 cup shortening, ½ cup finely chopped onion, and 3 cloves of finely chopped garlic.

Add 5 cups boiling water. Stir well and cover, simmering until meat is fork-tender (about two hours). Then blend in left-over flour mix. Add 12 medium carrots sliced into 1″ slices, 6 medium potatoes quartered, #2 can of onions, 3 tsp celery seed. Cover and simmer another 30 minutes or until vegetables are tender. Add 1 pkg of frozen peas (10 oz.). Serves 12 to 15.

—*Elizabethtown (Pennsylvania) Church of the Brethren*

was reversed. The tables had to be positioned, washed, and covered with a clean white tablecloth.

Communion was held, men on the east side, women on the west. The communion meat was cooked outside, in a large iron kettle, heated by a wood fire, at the rear of the church. The communion meat (beef) was purchased usually in a quarter or a quarter and a one-half slab. Before the start of the service, the men formed a line alternating from side to side passing the pans of communion meat to the deacons who placed it on the tables. This was done in silence, very sanctimoniously.

Once the participants were seated, communion began, usually led by a minister, elder, or visiting dignitary. On the tablecloths were placed plates (graniteware), spoons, plates of bread, tin cups, serving dishes of communion meat (covered by plates), pitchers of water, two glasses of grape juice, and two plates of communion bread. The table was covered with a second tablecloth.

Participants were seated, six to each side of a table, twelve to a table. When communion was served it was always to the participant's left. Under the table on the flat board bracing the legs were songbooks to be used in the service. Also at the ends of each table on the floor was a foot tub with warm water, a wash basin, a towel, and an apron. . . .

Once everyone had their feet and hands washed, scripture related to the Last Supper was read to begin the meal. The food was blessed. The presiding minister ordered the tables to be uncovered. The smell of beef and broth permeated the air. Although the minister usually told the congregation to eat supper at home before coming to communion, the trick of loving beef and broth was abstaining from eating supper. To the beef broth were added a few pieces of bread to make sop which was very tasty. Many Brethren looked forward to the love feast because they relished the food (and still do). Although the presiding elder described

it as a "token meal," it was anything but that. Many hungrily ate
of it in the time allotted.

The top tablecloth was
ceremoniously shuffled back and
forth, uncovering and covering
the table. This was done by
orders of the presiding minister.
This process required the
participation of everyone as each
person held the cloth over the
tops of the tableware and passed
it back and forth over the
table. . . .

At some communions, a
small table was set up for the
children. They partook of the
"Lord's Supper," but not of the
[bread and cup]. Nonmembers, visitors, and children were allowed
to sit in the balcony where they watched proceedings. At that time
Brethren did not practice "open" communion; now any believing
Christian can participate. . . .

At one communion an unusually hungry child continued to eat,
clanking his spoon after all had eaten. An uneasy silence fell over the
room as leaders at the head table started to squirm. All eyes were
fixed on the ravishly eating child. He looked about and wondered
why all the attention. He is a grown man now and still likes to eat!

—*Willis Hershberger,* Through the Years at Elkhart Valley Church of the Brethren

They also declared that the sum total of their guilt or error
amounted to no more than this: they had met regularly before
dawn on a fixed day to chant verses alternately among
themselves in honour of Christ as if to a god, and also to bind
themselves by an oath, not for any criminal purpose, but to
abstain from theft, robbery, and adultery, to commit no breach
of trust and not to deny a deposit when called upon to restore
it. After this ceremony it had been their custom to disperse and
reassemble later to take food of an ordinary, harmless kind.

This made me decide it was all the more necessary to
extract the truth by torture from two slave-women, whom they
call deaconesses.

—*Pliny (c. 112),* Letters and Panegyricus, *Loeb Classical Library, vol. 2*

On the first day of Unleavened Bread, when the Passover lamb is sacrificed, his disciples said to him, "Where do you want us to go and make the preparations for you to eat the Passover?" So he sent two of his disciples, saying to them, "Go into the city, and a man carrying a jar of water will meet you; follow him, and wherever he enters, say to the owner of the house, 'The Teacher asks, Where is my guest room where I may eat the Passover with my disciples?' He will show you a large room upstairs, furnished and ready. Make preparations for us there." So the disciples set out and went to the city, and found everything as he had told them; and they prepared the Passover meal.

When it was evening, he came with the twelve. And when they had taken their places and were eating, Jesus said, "Truly I tell you, one of you will betray me, one who is eating with me." They began to be distressed and to say to him one after another, "Surely, not I?" He said to them, "It is one of the twelve, one who is dipping bread into the bowl with me. For the Son of Man goes as it is written of him, but woe to that one by whom the Son of Man is betrayed! It would have been better for that one not to have been born."

—Mark 14:12-21

The agape meal is rich in its simplicity, often consisting of just meat, broth, and bread. The only utensils necessary are bowls and spoons. Photo by Phil Grout.

COMMUNION

For as this bread was once scattered over the mountains but was brought together into one loaf, so too gather our fellowship from the four corners of the world into your kingdom.

—*Didache*

EATING TOGETHER is important. In the Bible, meals are often used to include outsiders, as when Jesus eats with Zacchaeus. They describe the coming kingdom, as with the wedding feast. And they signify unity of the body, as with the feeding of the multitudes. In the end these are all examples of meals that unified the body of believers. The other type of meal, the Eucharist, is communion, in which all eat and drink to remember Jesus Christ. Jesus himself commands the practice, saying "eat my body broken for you; drink my blood shed for you."

In the early church, the agape meal was used to celebrate and, indeed, form community among believers and to unify them into the body of Christ. At the same time, the Eucharist was a meal to celebrate and remember Jesus Christ who redeemed and reconciled the people to God. It was not a full meal but a symbolic one consisting of the bread, representing the body of Christ broken to save the world, and the cup, representing the blood of Christ shed for us. In the fifth century, the agape meal disappeared as a formal practice in the church, leaving the Eucharist as the central part of Christian worship. It has survived to the present as the mass.

In high church traditions, Christ is present to believers in the substance of the bread and the wine. Brethren believe, however, that Christ is present in the church body or "where two or three are gathered in my name, I am there among them" (Matt. 18:20). Brethren do not practice communion as a sacrament, but as an ordinance or a commandment. Jesus commanded that we eat and drink to remember him and to be reconciled to God. Furthermore, the bread and the cup are not the actual body and blood of Christ, but symbols pointing to the great truth that God is with us in all of life.

Chinese Brethren in Tsinchow hold their first love feast, December 9, 1933. Photo by Ernest Wampler (BHLA Collection).

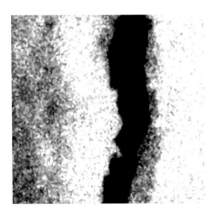

Early Brethren looked to the Gospel and Epistle accounts of the Eucharist and came to choose unleavened bread and the "fruit of the vine" as the most faithful response to the command. Wine was used until the temperance movement of the late nineteenth and early twentieth centuries, whereupon it was replaced with unfermented grape juice. The Brethren who argued that alcohol was "of the devil" finally won out, though not without much debate, over the literalists who saw no reason to take what was commanded in the Bible as evil.

For many years Brethren shared the wine from a common cup, for Jesus said, "Take this [cup] and divide it among yourselves" (Luke 22:17). Today, for the most part, the wine is divided into individual communion cups, mostly for reasons of sanitation.

The greatest change, however, has come for women. Until 1910, brothers broke bread between each other, but deacons served each woman the bread and the cup individually. Deacons would pass behind a row of women, handing each one first a piece of bread over her shoulder, and then the cup, which she handed back to the deacon instead of to the sister at her side. Through the persistent efforts of Julia Gilbert over a period of about fifty years, the practice was changed so that women now break their own bread, just as they wash one another's feet and share the kiss.

The placement of communion at the end of the love feast is more a matter of biblical interpretation than of order of importance. In the Gospel accounts, the feast of remembrance comes at the end of the last supper. For Brethren, the agape meal has grown to be at least as central, because it takes into account both the unity of the community and the remembrance of Christ as he is present in the ones gathered. As Brethren became less sectarian in the twentieth century, however, some congregations began to call for communion during worship, apart from the love feast. Once again, there was great debate, which, as was usual for Brethren, was resolved by allowing those congregations to have communion in the pew, if they wished. Those who hold to the traditional way do not practice communion apart from the full love feast.

In both cases, for love feast or for communion alone, the people who prepare the bread and cup prepare them in a worshipful manner. There are often devotions before the deacons set about to make the bread, a process

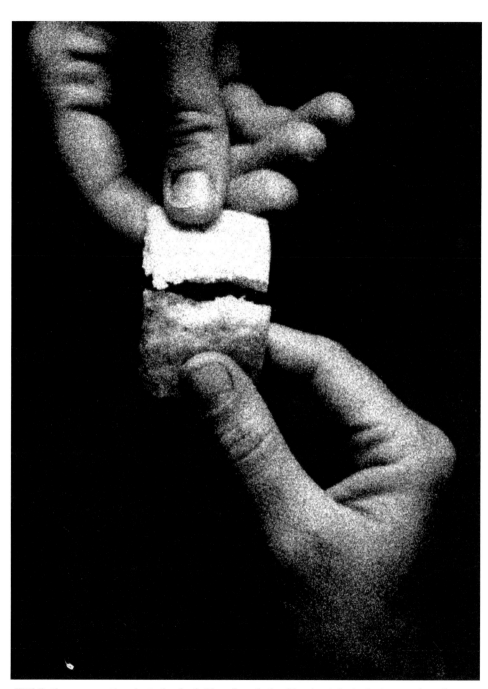

Bread of life, whose body, broken,
Feeds the hunger of my heart,
May the thanks that you have spoken
Bless each loaf I break apart.

Let these hands now calmly folding
Speak my gratitude for grace
Lest the treasure I am holding
Disappear before my face.

Lord, I welcome you to table;
Grace my supper ever new.
With your feast of love enable
Every guest to live for you.

—*Kenneth I. Morse (1952)*

"While they were eating, he took a loaf of bread, and after blessing it he broke it, gave it to them, and said, 'Take; this is my body' " (Mark 14:22). BHLA Collection.

We didn't take part as children until we were baptized, but we loved that communion bread, so we would sneak in after the communion was all done to get some, which was wrong. We weren't supposed to, but it was good. It was like a short-bread. I'm not sure it had some sugar in it.

—*Ruth Fillmore, Buffalo Grove, Illinois*

that takes an hour to knead in some cases. The bread is rich, a sort of short-bread. To some it would seem like a dessert. It is in the coming together of the body of Christ that makes it more than a confection. It is a meaningful, holy symbol of the broken body of Jesus and our own brokenness, ever ready for reconciliation with God.

On occasions other than communion, people have been known to make the bread for a treat. One man from Los Angeles solved the problem of not getting enough communion bread to satisfy himself by taking the Ladera Church of the Brethren recipe and making himself a batch. Then he ate the whole thing. It's all part of the paradox of being a non-sacramental church. The things themselves are not holy, even if, at times, they are kept separate for baptized believers. They're just bread and grape juice and meat and broth. It's in the act of sharing together that the holiness resides.

The bread

Historically, the Brethren and other Anabaptist groups reject the doctrine of Transubstantiation that holds that Christ is actually present in the bread. When scripture says, "Take, eat; this is my body" (Matt. 26:26), Brethren regard the bread only as a symbol and hold that this belief does not diminish it's importance. Tradition varies in local churches, but generally women deacons will meet in the church kitchen several days before communion to bake unleavened bread.

Deacons make a rich dough of flour, sugar, cream, and salt, pressing it into large shallow pans. The unbaked dough is scored into strips for easy cutting after baking. Using a fork or homemade implement, deacons poke rows of holes in the dough (five holes for the five wounds of Christ on the cross, three holes for the trinity, or twelve holes in each piece for the disciples). Rows are spaced at half-inch intervals. After baking, the bread is divided into strips or at least two inches in length so that two people may break bread between them later at communion. The bread often breaks at a row of holes. In the ordinance of communion, a brief prayer of consecration is offered, after which the people recite the words of Apostle Paul, "The bread that we break, is it not a sharing in the body of Christ?" (1 Cor. 10:16). Communicants then break the bread and eat.

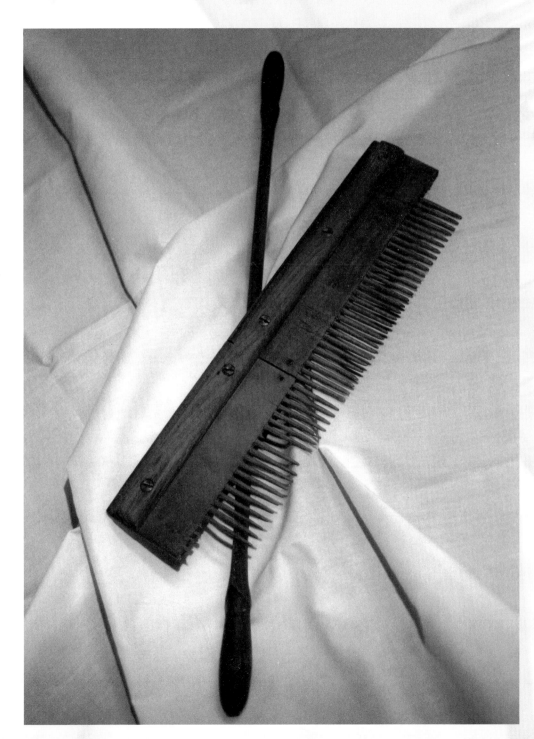

A member of the Beaver Creek congregation (Virginia) designed these implements for making communion bread when the congregation hosted Annual Meeting in 1861, moderated by John Kline. The comb simplified the process of perforating large quantities of bread, and the tapered rolling pin ensured a uniform thickness of the dough. *Photo by Regina Bryan.*

An Ancient Hebrew Communion Prayer

Blessed be the Lord Christ, the King of the Universe (who created all things), apportioned food, appointed dr[ink to all] the children of flesh in which they will be sat[isfied but gave to us] who are in the form of humans to eat from the food as to the numerous swarms of angels (and because of all this) we are led to bless in the raising of voice in the tumult (of people).

—Dura-Europos *Parchment D, 25.* *The prayer points to the existence of a Jewish Christian community that wrote in Hebrew in the late third century.*

In the believers church tradition, only those who profess their belief and have made a public commitment through baptism to follow Jesus are permitted to celebrate communion. The communion memories for many include the ways in which children, who were among those excluded, found ways to get a piece of bread. In some churches all the leftovers were set aside for children to eat later. Others report ways of surreptitiously including the children during the service by simply setting aside the "unbroken" pieces for the young ones sitting beside their parents or at a table for children. Since these pieces were not broken by brothers and sisters, they had not yet become communion bread.

Reuel Pritchett fondly remembered that "We children could eat the beef and soup at the meal, but of course we couldn't have the communion bread and the cup in the service. Afterwards, though, an old elder might break off for us pieces of that wonderful-tasting, unleavened bread and tell us something about its significance." In this way, the children who most certainly "belonged" to the community, though they were not members, could get a literal foretaste of church life. With this kind of nurture, they soon longed to become full members and full participants.

The cup

For the first 175 years, Brethren used homemade wine for communion, following the biblical example of Jesus and Paul. In the middle of the nineteenth century, Brethren backers of the prohibition movement called for unfermented grape juice as an option, but were completely rebuffed. Brethren leadership at Annual Conference in 1858 continued to counsel congregations to use "the purest article." But by 1875 Annual Meeting agreed to allow grape juice to be used as an alternative, despite strong objection from traditionalists. In his book *Brethren Society*, Carl Bowman notes the problem of reversing a time-honored, biblically based practice:

> On this issue, Isaac Price, a temperate brother from eastern Pennsylvania, pleaded in 1876 that the church permit those whose conscience forbade it to refrain from using fermented wine during communion. "Everybody agrees that alcohol produces evil, and only

This mug was used for love feast in the Germantown meetinghouse in the eighteenth century. The Germantown meetinghouse, built in 1770, is the oldest Brethren meetinghouse, and housed the first congregation in America. BHLA Collection.

evil," Price lamented; "I ask you, can the same cup represent both hell and heaven?" Such open expressions of conviction, though honest, sharply offended those who continued in the traditional practice. "It accuses us all of drinking the cup of devils," one brother raged, "we brethren that have tried to keep house after the ancient order . . . [it seems] that we have all the while been using the cup of devils. . . . Why if it was good for many years, to have pure wine at the communion, is it not good yet?" (112)

Unison: The bread which we break is the communion with the body of Christ.

Jesus says: "Take and eat. This is my body which is broken for you. Do this in remembrance of me."

Unison: The cup which we drink is the communion of the blood of Christ.

Jesus says: "Drink it, all of you. . . . This is my blood which seals God's covenant, my blood poured out for many for the forgiveness of sins. Do this in remembrance of me."

Today, the custom is almost universal to use unfermented grape juice. And since the elements are symbolic for Brethren, a symbol of the wine is sufficient. Except where a common cup is used today, each table at love feast is furnished with small glasses of grape juice. Following brief remarks and a prayer of consecration, each member repeats the words of Apostle Paul, "The cup of blessing which we bless, is it not the communion of the blood of Christ?" (1 Cor. 10:16). While drinking, members are encouraged to consider that the wine represents the shed blood of Jesus Christ and are asked to reflect on the price of his sacrificial death that has reconciled us to God. "For as often as ye eat this bread, and drink this cup, ye do shew the Lord's death till he come" (1 Cor. 11:26 KJV). *F.R.*

When the hour came, he took his place at the table, and the apostles with him. He said to them, "I have eagerly desired to eat this Passover with you before I suffer; for I tell you, I will not eat it until it is fulfilled in the kingdom of God." Then he took a cup, and after giving thanks he said, "Take this and divide it among yourselves; for I tell you that from now on I will not drink of the fruit of the vine until the kingdom of God comes." Then he took a loaf of bread, and when he had given thanks, he broke it and gave it to them, saying, "This is my body, which is given for you. Do this in remembrance of me." And he did the same with the cup after supper, saying, "This cup that is poured out for you is the new covenant in my blood. But see, the one who betrays me is with me, and his hand is on the table. For the Son of Man is going as it has been determined, but woe to that one by whom he is betrayed!" Then they began to ask one another, which one of them it could be who would do this.

A dispute also arose among them as to which one of them was to be regarded as the greatest. But he said to them, "The kings of the Gentiles lord it over them; and those in authority over them are called benefactors. But not so with you; rather the greatest among you must become like the youngest, and the leader like one who serves. For who is greater, the one who is at the table or the one who serves? Is it not the one at the table? But I am among you as one who serves.

—Luke 22:14-27

135

Communion Bread.—Take 1½ pints of sweet cream, butter the size of two eggs, ½ cup of white sugar, and flour enough to make about like pie dough. Bake in sheets, marking each sheet into strips and piercing the strips with a fork before baking. Flat sheets of tin kept for the purpose are nice for baking it on.—Sister E. S. Moore, Eldora, Iowa. (*Inglenook Cook Book*)

Communion Bread.—Take 3 pints of milk and 1 pound of butter, and as much flour as to give it a body similar to pie dough. Divide it into 4 parts and work each part until it blisters; then roll out till about the thickness of pie dough. Lay it off with a ruler an inch broad into inch strips, at the same time cutting the creases or divisions about half the thickness of the cake. Perforate each strip with 2 rows of holes from end to end and then bake. This will make enough for 250 members.—Sister Sadie K. Imler, Ridgely, Maryland. (*Inglenook Cook Book*)

Communion Bread

6 cups flour

2 tablespoons sugar

½ lb butter

½ pint whipping cream.

Sift flour and mix sugar in a large bowl. Cut in butter until it forms a fine meal-like texture. Stir in whipping cream. Mixture will be very stiff and crumbly. Divide into four parts and knead ½ hour on a lightly floured board. Preheat oven to 400. Spread dough evenly about 3/8" thick on 2 flat cookie sheets. Score into 3/4" squares and prick each section with fork tines. Reduce oven temperature at 300 when cookie sheets are put in. Bake at least 1 hour (will not look real done as it does not brown). Cut immediately along scored lines into single or double sections, depending on the service.

—*Ladera Church of the Brethren, Los Angeles, California*

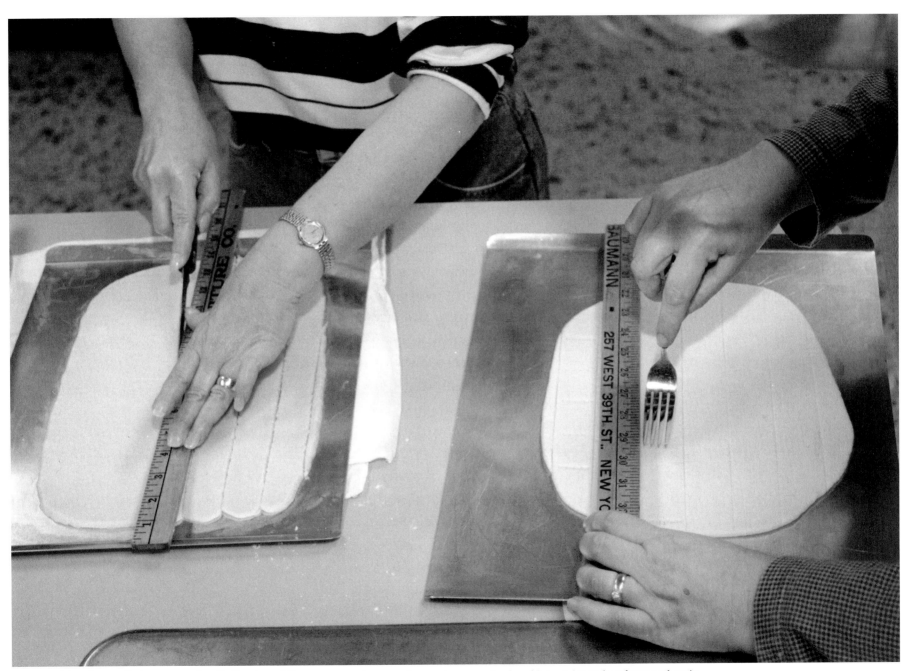

Women of the Pleasant Dale congregation (Indiana) carefully measure and score unleavened communion bread into strips and perforate each strip for breaking. A fifth hole is added alongside the four tine holes to symbolize the five wounds of Jesus on the cross. Photo by Regina Bryan.

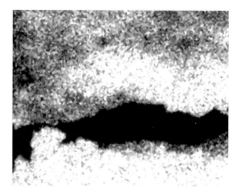

 If anything, dogmatic assertions of real presence are in danger of detracting from examination of confirming signs of whether Christ really is present—in signs of love of the brothers and sisters, turning from sin, commitment to lives of self-sacrifice, and the like.

—*Marlin Jeschke, in* The Lord's
   Supper: Believers Church
   Perspectives

 Traditionally, in making the love feast bread, they would put rows of five holes, five punctures, across the strips.

During my youth, we had these old bone handled knives and forks, which were two hundred years old, to make the row of five punctures. They would make one with a two tine, and then another, and that would give four, and for the next one they would take the fork and put one puncture mark, and the other tine would go into the scoring between strips. Apparently in other congregations they got a local craftsman to make a five-tine fork that would make the perfect row.

It was always explained that the five holes were to memorialize the five wounds Christ received on the cross, and when the portion of the bread was broken to us and everyone was served, an elder would say something about the significance of the bread.

We always broke our individual piece of bread into five pieces, and we would eat each piece separately, and again we were told that was symbolic of the five wounds of Christ.

—*Clarence Kulp, Harleysville, Pennsylvania*

When he was at the table with them, he took bread, blessed
and broke it, and gave it to them. Then their eyes were opened,
and they recognized him; and he vanished from their sight.
They said to each other, "Were not our hearts burning within
us while he was talking to us on the road, while he was
opening the scriptures to us?"
—*Luke 24:30-32*

*Communion with the risen Lord happens in many places. The disciples met the risen Christ on
the road to Emmaus and broke bread with him, whereupon their eyes were opened. Brethren
young people walk with Christ on a march through the Shenandoah Valley, witnessing to the
gospel message of peace and justice.* Photo by David Radcliff.

Here at Blue River years ago the grape juice was homemade. Once it was not quite the right color in the opinion of the deacons' wives. The pastor's wife ran over to the parsonage and returned with blue food coloring, which was added to the grape juice. It had a marvelous color. We thought nothing more of it until after communion when we noticed that everyone's lips and tongues were a nice color of blue.

—*Craig Alan Myers,*
Columbia City, Indiana

Until the late nineteenth century, communicants drank from a common cup, such as these pewter cups from the Heidelberg meetinghouse (Pennsylvania). Photo by E. G. Hoff (BHLA Collection).

In one of the least biblical aspects of early Brethren communion, women were not allowed to break bread or pass the cup to each other during the final portion of the love feast. An elder had to go from woman to woman, first breaking bread with each individually, then offering the cup. He walked behind the women, reaching over each one's shoulder with the bread and then the cup, which each handed back to him in turn.

In 1849 a query questioned Annual Meeting as to whether it wouldn't be more biblically consistent for women to break bread and share the cup among themselves, as was practiced among the men. The query was denied. In 1857 the question was raised again.

1857

Why do not the sisters break the bread, and pass the cup to each other, in the same manner as the brethren do at the communion?

Answer: Man being the head of the woman, and it having been the practice of the church, from time immemorial, for the officiating brethren to break the bread to the sisters, we know of no scriptural reason for making a change in our practice.

—*Annual Meeting minutes, 1857,* Full Report

We shared a common cup of grape juice that we called wine. I don't know if we still have any of the glasses we used. They were cut glass, in an elaborate pattern, almost out of place in the stark simplicity of the service. The bread, in long uncut strips, was broken and passed along the table. I think it was Anna Strycker who suggested a few years back that we serve bread that way again. Unfortunately, when we got involved in symbolism and phrases and blessings and making sure we did it just right, we lost the meaning of that element of communion.

—*Pearl Aldrich,*
North Liberty, Indiana

Brethren have served communion from simple vessels made of wood and metal and from ornate cups and pitchers like these porcelain and cut glass items from the Pleasant Dale meetinghouse (Indiana). Photo by Regina Bryan.

1883

The Scriptures no where say whether sisters should break the bread of communion, or have it broken to them; hence it remains one of the questions that must be settled by the spirit of the gospel.

1. It should be remembered that under the law, women were excused from all military duty; neither did they serve in the priest's office; besides women were not allowed to go beyond the court of women, toward the holy house of the temple.
2. Under the gospel, woman is not "to usurp authority," but to be "in subjection." Neither Christ nor the apostles ever called woman to positions of authority in the church, hence do not administer, but are administered unto; and like under the law, they in the meantime share all the benefits of the gospel. I therefore conclude from the spirit of the above scriptures, that sisters should not break bread, but have the bread broken to them.

—I. J. Rosenberger, Brethren at Work, May 1883

From New Lebanon, Montgomery Co., O.—July 23, 1883
Dear Brethren:—
If Bro. I. J. Rosenberger's conclusion is right in the last *Brethren at Work* about sisters not breaking bread, would someone be so kind as to instruct us sisters what conclusion to come to, when we are administering the ordinance of feet-washing, and the salutation of the holy kiss to one another around the table of the Lord? I hope I am not out of place by asking this question.

—Julia A. Gilbert, The Gospel Messenger, *June 23, 1883*

Like the widow before the judge, Julia A. Gilbert had a great desire to resolve a burning issue. From the time she was baptized in 1858, she wondered why women had to be served by the men at communion. In 1910, Annual Meeting gave women the privilege of serving communion to each other, largely by the tireless efforts of Julie Gilbert.
Converse photo (BHLA Collection).

I was born Jan. 27, 1844, near the foot of South Mountain, Frederick Co., Md. My parents, two brothers, and I, and a young man named Isaiah Gross, came to the neighborhood, ten miles west of Dayton, Ohio, in a two-horse wagon. I think I was in my fourth year. We were about seventeen days on the road. I was about eight years old when I began thinking about living the Christian life, when I would be old enough. At that time it was a question as to how old a child should be until it can unite with the church.

In 1850 I attended the Annual Meeting for the first time. It was about five miles from our home. I remember seeing the long tables at the communion, and the many teams. When I was past eleven years of age, I was taken with measles and scarlet fever, which caused me to become a cripple for life. A brother and a sister of mine died in one day. At the age of fourteen I was baptized by Eld. Abram Erbaugh, in the Wolf Creek congregation. At that time I was the only single member in the church at that place, so far as I knew, but others soon came into the fold. I went on my way, rejoicing until I attended the love feast and took my first communion. Then I was puzzled.

At that time there was no supper on the tables at the time of feet-washing. As I thought about how the Savior rose from supper, laid aside his garments and girded himself, I pondered for several days, with the Testament in my hand, at my work. At last I concluded I would ask my father, as he was a great lover of his Bible. I think I can almost see him yet, as he sat on a low rocking-chair, when I read the passage in question and asked him why the members did that way at the love feast. He gave a heavy sigh and said: "The old brethren took the ordinance from several passages of Scripture and thought this to be the proper way it ought to be done."

This explanation gave me satisfaction for a while, but when I thought of the vow that I had made to God, to walk in all his ways (and our aged Brethren used to teach that it was Christ whom we should follow), and read the Scriptures, I felt that it was my duty to see if we were doing things in the way Christ told us to do them. Next came the breaking of bread for the sisters, and then I had another struggle. I told Bro. Lewis W. Teeter, in 1894, when talking on the subject, that I then thought if the Lord would let me live to have that experience,—breaking the bread and passing the cup,—he ought to take me home, as I thought I had fought enough battles. But it went on a great while longer than they, at that time, thought it would. It seems the Lord must have had something for me to do in this world.

—*Julia Gilbert,* The Gospel Messenger, *July 13, 1912*

This illustration for The Gospel Messenger *(Nov. 4, 1911) illustrates men serving bread to both the women and the men at love feast.*

1894

Dear Brethren, we, the sisters of the Wolf Creek Church, seeing that we have made the same covenant with God in Christ Jesus that you made, we petition Annual Meeting through district meeting to repeal your former decisions against us and grant us the same privilege in the breaking of bread and passing the cup as you do the brethren.

—*Query to church council, Wolf Creek, 1894. Cited in* Messenger, *June 1976*

[Twice Julia Gilbert's query was denied. Upon the death of her parents, Julia moved in 1897 to Grundy County, Iowa. A year later her query, with pretty much the exact same wording except for a change in the name of the church and the addition of a scriptural citation (1 Cor. 10:16), was accepted and passed along by the Old Grundy County German Baptist Church. By 1899 the query reached Annual Meeting where it was tabled for a year. From 1900 to 1910 it was the subject of consistent debate—and it was consistently delayed. The elders of the church, it seemed, weren't in any rush to make a decision.]

1900

We consider that this change would be in harmony with the teaching and example of Christ and also in harmony with the practice of the church during the apostolic period.

—*Report of original committee, D. Hays, L. W. Teeter, I. B. Trout,*
Annual Meeting 1900, Full Report

I do not know, but I believe it would be better not to hurry this matter too fast.

—*M. J. McClure, Annual Meeting 1900,* Full Report

I am in favor of deferring this question for one year because that is the principle that our brethren have always adopted when there was not a union of sentiment, and especially when it came to making a change, a change in something so important as the Communion. The truth will not lose anything by so deferring it. The result of this I am sure will be to unify us more and we cannot lose anything by doing that; therefore I am in favor of deferring it and spreading it on the Minutes so we can give it another year's thought.

—*Daniel Vaniman, Annual Meeting 1900,* Full Report

I do not propose to make a speech or any explanation more than this, that we did not anticipate the passage of the paper, and I believe, if I remember rightly, we did not even desire the passage of our paper to-day, but we preferred that you might have a year to consider this question, which, as the brother says, involves a change. Of course I am decidedly in favor of the answer to that paper, although when I started to investigate it I was decidedly opposed to the answer, and I did not expect to arrive at any such conclusion, but in spite of traditional rubbish or anything else I was bound to come to a Gospel conclusion. Now let us weigh it for one year and vote it through next year unanimously.

—*I. B. Trout, Annual Meeting 1900,* Full Report

. . . I would unhesitatingly say to-day that we would not offend the dignity of heaven or of God or the Lord Jesus Christ or the Holy Spirit if we would make that change today, but I say it looks to me that it is possible we might offend the dignity of some of our dear brethren, and in consequence of that fact I favor the idea of deferring for a year.

—*J. B. Light, Annual Meeting 1900,* Full Report

As Brethren became aware of the health dangers of sharing a common cup, the tradition gave way to individual servings. Women drink the cup during love feast at the Mt. Carmel congregation in Virginia. *Photo by J. Henry Long (BHLA Collection).*

One year later . . . 1901

J. M. Neff: We should all like to know what the Standing Committee has done with this paper [regarding communion].
Moderator (A. C. Wieand): It makes no difference. They did nothing.
—*Annual Meeting 1901,* Full Report

[There followed a long debate. But rather than allow the sisters to break bread, a substitute motion was made that bread be broken for both brothers and sisters alike. This was bound to be unpopular with men.]

Moderator (A. C. Wieand): We want to put the motion now. The motion is that we pass the answer of the committee. What will you have if this motion prevails? If this motion prevails, then the administrator will break the bread to both the brethren and sisters alike. That is what you will have. Are you ready for the question? [Cries of question.] All who are in favor of the motion, make it known by standing. All opposed to the motion, make it known by standing. That will do. The motion is lost. Now where are we? Just where we were before. The practice goes on just the same as we have had it.
—*A. C. Wieand, Annual Meeting 1901,* Full Report

[Over the next several years the question continued to be put off. In 1906 two motions were passed along to a Standing Committee subcommittee.]

 ## 1906

We recommend that these papers be placed in the hands of a committee of five to investigate the matter of breaking bread by sisters: first, as to its scriptural authority; second, as to its agreement with the practice of the primitive church; third, as it relates to the practice of the church during the past two hundred years, and to report to the Annual Meeting.

—*Report of the Annual Meeting 1906,* Full Report

 ## 1907

The report of the committee is as follows: "The matter is under investigation, but not ready for a report at this meeting."

—*E. B. Hoff, H. C. Early, A. G. Crosswhite, D. C. Flory, Annual Meeting 1907,* Full Report

 ## 1908

Conference appoints a committee and assigns them their duty, and they spend a year, and come up and say the matter is under investigation and they have nothing to report, and then we continue the committee another year, and they come up and say, that they were not able to get together, and now, shall we continue that same committee and recommit a question of some importance that our Brotherhood has been asking for an answer on for years?

—*I. D. Parker, Annual Meeting 1908,* Full Report

[Six pages of parliamentary discussion followed on whether the Annual Meeting was passing something or nothing, depending on whether the report was valid in the first place.]

One of two things,—either there is nothing before the house, or else this paper without an answer is before the house. If the paper without an answer is before the house, we will have to answer to dispose of it. To recommit it would even be in order. If nothing is before the house, the next thing to do is to pass on to something else. We are all agreed there is no answer before the house. The question I would like to ask, Is this paper here the property of Annual Meeting, or is it the property of this committee by the action of the last Conference?

—A. C. Wieand, *Annual Meeting 1908,* Full Report

[The paper was recommitted for one year.]

1910

As a church, we are, by no means, a unit on the question. In some churches the officiating brother breaks the bread to all of the sisters, but not to the brethren. Why is there a distinction? Secondly, in some churches,—and in a good many, I might say,—the practice is for the brethren to break the bread to each other, but when it comes to the sister, the officiating elder minister breaks the bread to a number of sisters, and then the sisters take it up, for a certain distance, and break to each other. Here is a variation in practice. . . . Now, in view of the fact that sisters already do break bread, and in view of the fact that all of the brethren break the bread to each other, it seems to me that we could be

more easily united, as a church, by granting to all the brethren and all the sisters the privilege of breaking bread.

—*J. T. Myers, Annual Meeting 1909,* Full Report

[The matter was deferred for one year.]

Your committee reports as follows; The officiating minister, or ministers, shall break the bread and pass the cup of communion to both brethren and sisters.

—*Committee Report, Annual Meeting 1910,* Full Report

[The parliamentary maneuvering began again—debate and delay. Then something extraordinary happened. Julia Gilbert, who rarely missed an Annual Meeting, finally got up and spoke. Hers was a rare female voice from the floor.]

I feel it my duty to give you a reason why we brought up this petition. I suppose if this decision that the brother spoke about, in 1857, had been always followed, you would never be bothered by this petition before this meeting or any other meeting. I think the brethren said what they wanted to say when the question was asked. What was the reason? It was said that man is the head of the woman. He is so, naturally, but he is not the spiritual head of the woman. When I came into the church, I was young, and when I took hold of our elder's hand and he led me into the water where there was a strong stream flowing, he said, "Don't be afraid, Jesus went before." And I walked down there, and between heaven and earth I made a covenant with God to live faithful

Jeanine Wine

to Christ Jesus until death. And didn't I come up out of the water the same as my dear Savior did? When we came to communion, didn't I rise from the supper the same as my Savior did? Didn't I gird myself the same as he did? Didn't I wash my sister's feet and thus obey the command to wash one another's feet? When we come down to the breaking of the bread and the passing of the cup, however, then man steps in between us and our Savior. Though man never suffered, or shed a drop of blood for us, he takes his hand to break the bread for us, as if God hadn't given us any hands. We have been using our hands right along, claiming to come in the Spirit, and following him. He brake the bread and gave unto them and said, "This do in remembrance of me." Of course I have been told there was no sister there. Well, there was no sister there in feet-washing. Excuse us from that if you want to use that scripture. But Paul comes to us with the words read at every communion. "Be ye followers of me as also I am of Christ." There were certainly sisters there, and Paul could tell them to be followers of him as he was of Christ. He followed Christ in breaking the bread, and therefore I think I have a right to ask these delegates to permit us sisters to break bread one to the other. We do not ask to break it to the brethren, but we want to fulfill that command, and be in touch with Jesus Christ. We want the letter and the spirit to go together.

—*Julia Gilbert, Annual Meeting 1910,* Full Report

I offer a substitute for the answer given, that we grant the sisters the same privilege of breaking the bread and passing the cup that brethren now enjoy.

—*E. G. Rodabaugh, Annual Meeting 1910,* Full Report

Jeanine Wine

Now, the motion is to pass the substitute. Are there any objections to the motion? [Cries of "Yes."] There is objection. We shall take a rising vote. All in favor of adopting the substitute, make it manifest by rising. All opposed rise. The substitute is passed.

—*I. W. Teeter, Acting Moderator, Annual Meeting 1910,* Full Report

[Julia Gilbert moved back to Ohio in 1918. She lived until the ripe age of 90 and died in 1927. She was able to enjoy her victory nearly a quarter of a century.]

The Tunker Love-Feast

Let us glance for a moment at one of those remarkable assemblies. Within the long, low auditorium a vast congregation, often numbering a thousand souls, throngs every foot of available space. The members are all seated around long, immaculately white tables. If it is a typical Tunker communion, the white caps of the sisters, framing pure and peaceful faces, ranged on either side of their separate tables, forms a picture which lingers long in the memory, in its unique and singular beauty. A narrow space along the walls of the church accommodates the audience, the outsiders, and thickly standing upon the benches which have been packed into this space, they gaze upon the scene before them with eager and unflagging interest, not seeming to be conscious of the long hours, nor of the fatigue attending their crowded and uncomfortable position. At a central table solemn and venerable men are conducting the service. A devout atmosphere pervades the house. The reverent voice of the officiating bishop arrests even the most careless ear, and all who are present feel that the place is holy, and that God Himself is not very far away.

The Tunker love-feast embraced a series of services, beginning usually on the forenoon of Saturday, and ending with a great assembly and a notable sermon on Sunday afternoon. If any other day was selected for opening, substantially the same course was pursued. The Saturday-forenoon service was followed by a dinner, which was served

to the whole congregation, having been prepared in the kitchen apartment. The young people belonging to the Tunker families in the community would assist in spreading the tables and waiting on the people. It was not unusual for the dinner to continue until three o'clock in the afternoon, and from three to nine hundred people were fed. The menu varied somewhat, according to the financial ability of the congregation. It invariably consisted of the very best bread, good butter, apple butter, pickles, and pies and coffee. If the church could afford it, fresh beef was also supplied.

Illustrating the fact that the throng is often hungrier for the loaves and fishes than for the spiritual gospel, it was often necessary to appoint door-keepers to regulate the crowd while the meal was in progress, and the strongest men in the community were chosen for this office. The recess following this meal was enjoyed by the members as a season of delightful social intercourse. In later years, however, this Saturday-morning sermon and dinner were abandoned by some congregations, and the services began with the "examination" in the afternoon,—a season of devout seriousness, a spiritual preparation for the communion proper,—which was soon to follow.

1 Cor. 11:38 was read as a basis for one or more discourses, after which the officiating elder would deliver an exhortation to prayer, being careful to remark in conclusion that there would be perfect freedom to any one, brother or sister, who might feel pressed to lead in open prayer, and the season would close with the Lord's Prayer. It was not unusual for three or four brethren to exercise in prayer, but it was very unusual to hear a sister pray on such or any other public occasion.

Then followed a short intermission after the announcement that the next service would be indicated by singing, when the members who expected to participate in the communion would take their seats on long benches at the tables immediately on entering the house, so that the deacons might know whether sufficient table-room had been prepared.

The song having been completed, the thirteenth chapter of John was read to the end of the thirtieth verse. After reading that scripture, with suitable admonition, the washing of feet began. Later on, the time for commencing the washing of feet was indicated when the reader came to the fourth verse, "He riseth from supper." At this point those who had been appointed to lead would arise, two by two, lay aside their garments, gird each other with a white apron, pour water into a small vessel, and proceed, one to wash and the other to wipe the feet of such persons as might be prepared to receive the service. The first two would wash and wipe the feet of from six to ten or more persons, when they would be relieved by such other two persons as might volunteer. This was called "the double mode." By "the single mode" one person arose, commenced the service by laying aside his coat, girding himself, and washing and wiping the feet of the member seated next to him. Then he gave the towel to the person whom he had served, who would proceed in the same manner to number three. Thus the work continued to the last one on the bench at a table, who, in turn, served number one.

After having washed and wiped the feet, the members engaged salute each other with the holy kiss. This custom is invariable among all denominations of Tunkers. In the Brethren congregations this is the only occasion when the salutation is ceremonially observed.

Clear water and clean towels are supplied for cleansing of hands. Besides the esthetic purpose, this washing of the hands indicates the sacredness of the succeeding ordinances of the Lord's Supper and the Communion.

Feet-washing having now been concluded, the Lord's Supper was next placed on the table. Certain ones had prepared the food during former exercises. It consisted of bread, mutton or beef, and soup made of meat broth. Thanks being offered, the meal was partaken of. After supper, during the singing of a hymn, the tables were cleared of every-

Jeanine Wine

thing except the cloths, which were turned. Then the Communion bread and wine were placed upon the table.

Then, usually, the nineteenth chapter of John was read, followed by a dissertation on the sufferings of Christ, by some preacher of merit, and closed by the elder, with an admonition to love and other duties. During this exhortation the elder prepared the Communion bread by breaking the loaves into narrow slices indicated by slight indentures before baking. These were placed side by side and crossed until the process was complete, and was performed with much exactness, and observed by all within sight with as much solemnity as the ordinance itself.

Then the salutation was introduced, quoting 1 Cor. 16:20, "Greet ye one another with an holy kiss," or kindred passages. Then the elder would extend his right hand to and kiss the brother next to him. Thus the salutation would pass to the last brother at the last table, who would kiss the officiating elder, thus completing the circle. After having started the divine command with the brethren, the elder in charge extended the right hand of fellowship to one of the sisters occupying an end of the table, with instructions to pass the salutation among themselves, and he followed the line to see that it was properly observed.

The following remarks were then made by the elder in charge. "The apostle Paul says, 'I have received of the Lord that which also I delivered unto you, that the Lord Jesus the same night in which He was betrayed took bread, and when He had given thanks, He brake it.' So, in like manner, we will also return thanks for this bread." Then all arose, and thanks were given for and a blessing asked upon the bread. After all were again seated, he proceeded. "The apostle says, 'The bread which we break, is it not the communion of the body of Christ,' which is equivalent to affirming that it is. So I will say to my brother, 'Beloved brother, the bread which we break is the communion of the body of Christ,'" and while speaking these words, he breaks a small piece from the long slice and hands it to him. The larger piece, from

"For as often as you eat this bread and drink the cup, you proclaim the Lord's death until he comes" (1 Cor. 11:26). *Illustration of communion by G. L. Croome in* Theological Writings *by Peter Nead, 1850.*

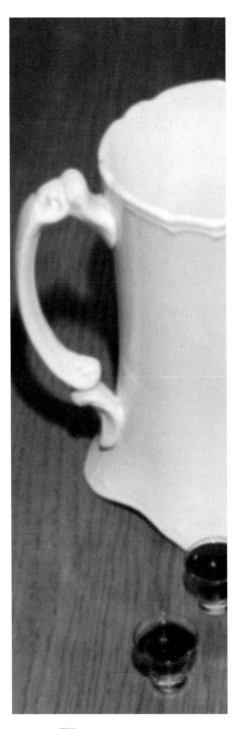

which he had broken, is passed to number two, who repeats the same to brother number three, etc. One or two sub-elders accompany the line with supplies of bread.

The leader then turns to the sister to whom he had extended the right hand of fellowship, saying "Beloved sister, the bread which we break is the communion of the body of Christ," breaking a piece and handing it to her. This he repeats substantially to the next sister, breaking bread for and to every sister at the table.

Both circles having completed the breaking of bread, the bishop remarks, "We have tarried one for another until all have been served, and we will now eat this bread, contemplating the sufferings of our Saviour." After all had eaten in silence, the white covering was removed from the wine, and two cups were filled. If several bottles were at hand, wine was poured from each one into each cup. This was done, we presume, to show that it was all alike . . ." After the same manner also He took the cup, when He had supped," is the bishop's next quotation, and he continues, "from which we conclude that as He had given thanks for the bread, He did also for the cup. Let us rise and give thanks for the cup."

When the members are seated again, he says, "Beloved brother, this cup of the New Testament is the communion of the blood of Christ," and hands a cup to whom he had broken bread; who, after taking a sip of the wine, passes it to the next brother, and so on until the circle is complete, the leader partaking last of all. A sub-elder follows the line with a supply, replenishing the cup when required.

The same quotation is repeated to the sisters, as the bishop hands the cup to the first one. After taking a sip, she returns the cup to the bishop, who hands it to the next sister, and so on until all have been served. No matter how inconvenient it may be for the leader to give and have returned to him, the cup must be given to each sister by the officiating elder. This has been an inflexible rule with the German

Baptist and Old German Baptist branches of the Tunker fraternity, to the close of the nineteenth century.

During the passing of the cup the congregation engages in singing, but during the breaking of bread singing is not generally permitted.

The last quotation, to close the Communion, is now repeated: "And they sang a hymn and went out." This is followed by prayer and song, and the congregation may consider itself dismissed.

—*Henry Holsinger in* History of the Tunkers

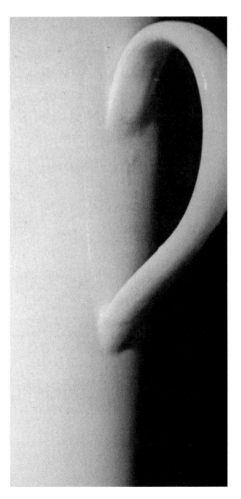

After the feetwashing and the love feast, time for the [bread and cup] began. Brethren at the head table would take turns reading the appropriate scripture. The presiding minister would then rise with the bread or the cup and state what he wanted the participants to repeat after him. "The bread which we bless is the communion of the body of Christ," and "The cup that we bless is the communion of the blood of Christ." Brethren do not condone the drinking of wine, consequently participants drank grape juice.

In the ceremony of the bread, the same procedure used in feetwashing applied. The end person to the right reached under the top tablecloth and picked up the plate of unleavened bread. It was cut into inch strips and marked with a fork prick where it should be broken for each participant. The baking of the bread was done using a prescribed recipe, in a deaconess' home aided by other deaconesses.

The end person then broke a portion and handed it to the one to the left. This was repeated around the table. The presiding minister then ordered, "Eat ye all of it." If the person on the right broke off a large piece for a neighbor or if the bread was dry and eating it was a prob-

lem, the neighbor could wash it down with the tin cup of water or slip it into a pocket.

After the blessing of the cup, the one on the end would reach under the top tablecloth and secure the tumbler filled with grape juice. This person would not drink of it; but rather passed it to the neighbor on the left who took a sip, then passed it on round the table. (The end person, despairing of finding a clean spot on the tumbler head, took only a sip and replaced it under the top tablecloth as the minister admonished, "Drink ye all of it."

After the communion ceremony the participants sang a hymn and went home. Not true! Just the visitors. The tables had to be cleared and replaced in the basement. The church floor had to be mopped. The benches had to be replaced for Sunday worship. The surplus meat and broth were placed in mason jars and given or sold to members. (A tradition which still occurs.) During the ceremony, water was being heated in the large iron kettle to wash the tableware. Tablecloths, aprons, and towels were taken home by the deaconesses to be laundered.

—*Willis Hershberger,* Through the Years at Elkhart Valley Church of the Brethren

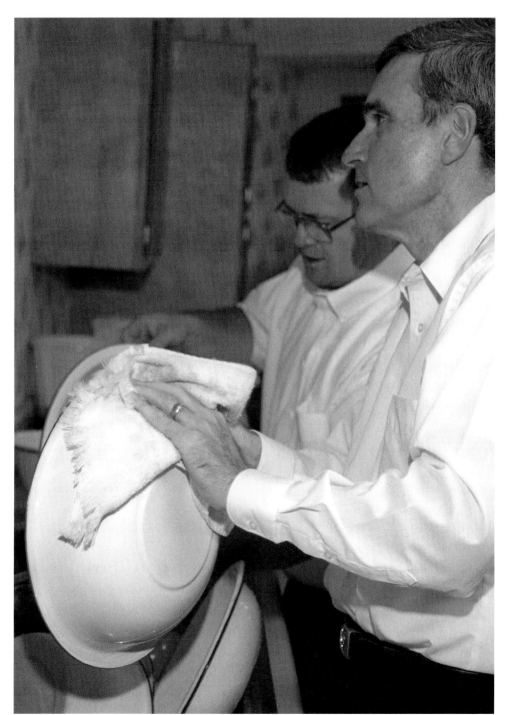

Love feast does not end with communion but with the mundane task of washing dishes, moving tables and chairs, laundering linens, sweeping the floor, and parceling out leftovers. The unity required to hold love feast carries the community through the last chore and into the daily tasks of church life. Photo by Regina Bryan.

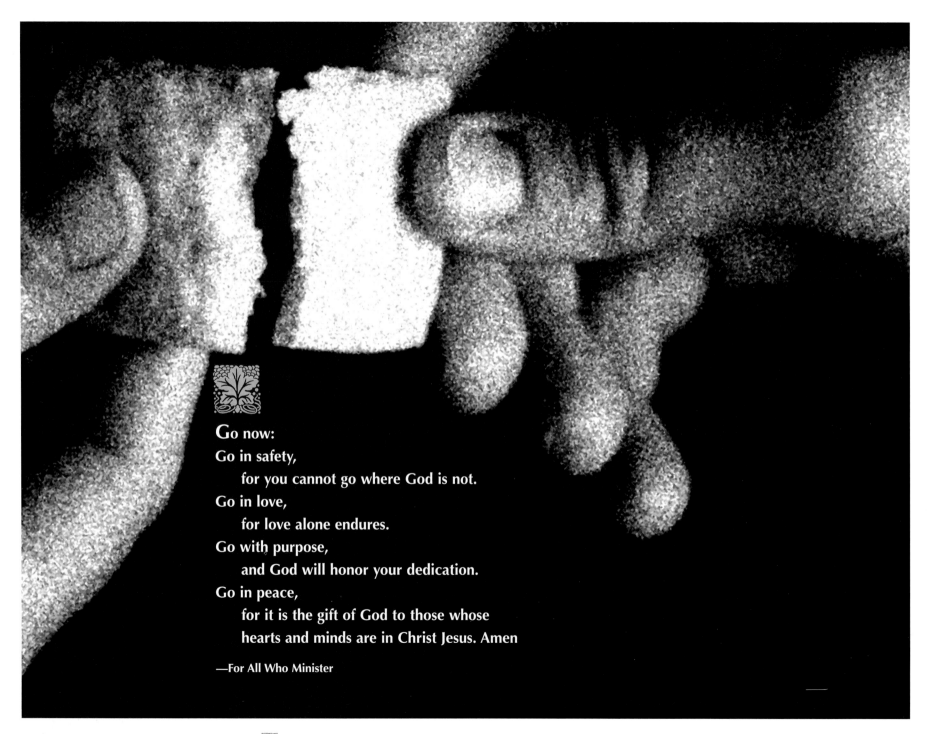

Go now:

Go in safety,
   for you cannot go where God is not.

Go in love,
   for love alone endures.

Go with purpose,
   and God will honor your dedication.

Go in peace,
   for it is the gift of God to those whose
   hearts and minds are in Christ Jesus. Amen

—For All Who Minister

BIBLIOGRAPHY

A Collection of Hymns and Sacred Songs (Old German Baptist Church), 1882.

Arnold's Grove/Mount Carroll (Illinois) Council Meeting Minutes, 1874-1932. BHLA Collection.

Bowman, Carl F. and Stephen L. Longenecker, eds. *Anabaptist Currents*. Bridgewater, Va.: Forum for Religious Studies, 1995.

Bowman, Carl F. *Brethren Society*. Baltimore: Johns Hopkins University Press, 1995.

Brethren at Work. Mt. Morris, Ill.: 1883. BHLA Collection.

Brethren Historical Library and Archives, 1451 Dundee Avenue, Elgin, Illinois 60120.

Brethren Life and Thought. Summer 1964; Summer 1965; Summer 1967; Spring/Summer 1996. Brethren Journal Association and Bethany Theological Seminary.

Brumbaugh, H. B. *The Brethren's Church Manual*. Mt. Morris, Ill.: Brethren's Publishing Company, 1887.

Chrysostom, St. John. *Commentary on Saint John the Apostle and Evangelist*, Homilies 48-88. Thomas A. Goggin, tr. Washington, D.C.: Catholic University Press, 1960.

Durnbaugh, Hedwig T. *The German Hymnody of the Brethren 1720-1903*. Philadelphia: The Brethren Encyclopedia, Inc., 1986.

Durnbaugh, Donald F., comp. *European Origins of the Brethren*. Elgin, Ill.: Brethren Press, 1958.

Durnbaugh, Donald F. *Fruit of the Vine*. Elgin, Ill.: Brethren Press, 1997.

Durnbaugh, Donald F., ed. *The Brethren in Colonial America*. Elgin, Ill.: Brethren Press, 1967.

Eberly, William R., ed. *The Complete Writings of Alexander Mack*. Winona Lake, Ind.: BMH Books, 1991.

Eby, Kermit. *For Brethren Only*. Elgin, Ill.: Brethren Press, 1958.

Eller, Vernard. *In Place of Sacraments*. Grand Rapids: Eerdmans, 1972.

For All Who Minister: A Worship Manual for the Church of the Brethren. Elgin, Ill.: Brethren Press, 1993.

Full Report. Church of the Brethren Annual Meeting minutes for 1857, 1888, 1895, 1900, 1901, 1906- 1910. BHLA Collection.

Gibble, Kenneth L. *Once Upon a Wonder: Imaginings from the Gospels*. Nashville: Upper Room Books, 1992.

Gibble, June A., and Fred W. Swartz. *Called to Caregiving*. Elgin, Ill.: Brethren Press, 1987.

Gibbons, Phebe. *The Plain People in Pennsylvania Dutchland*. Lebanon, Pa.: Applied Arts Publishers, 1963.

Gospel Messenger. June 23, 1883; July 13, 1912. Elgin, Ill.: The Brethren Publishing House.

Hawthorne, Gerald H. *Philippians* (Word Biblical Commentary). Nashville: Word Publishing, 1983.

Hershberger, Willis. *Through the Years at Elkhart Valley Church of the Brethren*. Privately printed, 1991.

Holsinger, Henry R. *History of the Tunkers and the Brethren Church*. Privately printed, 1901.

Inglenook Cook Book. Elgin, Ill.: Brethren Press, 1911.

Loeb Classical Library, Vol. 2. Cambridge: Harvard University Press, 1969.

Messenger. April 1, 1971; June 1976. Elgin, Ill.: Church of the Brethren General Board.

Montel, Wanda, and Mary Montel, Helen Lechrone, Mabel Freed, comps. *History of the Eel River (Indiana) Church of the Brethren, 1838-1988*. Privately printed.

Morse, Kenneth I. *Listen to the Sunrise*. Elgin, Ill.: Brethren Press, 1991.

Pennsylvania Folklife, Winter 1991-92. Collegeville, Pa.: Pennsylvania Folklife Society.

Pritchett, Reuel B., with Dale Aukerman. *On the Ground Floor of Heaven*. Elgin, Ill.: Brethren Press, 1980.

Roberts, Alexander, and James Donaldson, eds. *Ante-Nicene Fathers*, Vols. IV, V. Grand Rapids, Mich.: Eerdmans.

Schaff, Philip, and Henry Wace, eds. *Nicene and Post-Nicene Fathers*, Vol. X. Grand Rapids, Mich.: Eerdmans, 1955.

Stoffer, Dale R., ed. *The Lord's Supper: Believers Church Perspectives*. Scottdale, Pa.: Herald Press, 1997.

Thomas, John Christopher. *Footwashing in John 13 and the Johannine Community*. Sheffield, Eng.: Sheffield Academic Press, 1991.

Two Centuries of the Church of the Brethren: Bicentennial Addresses, 1909.

Zug, R. *History of the Church of the Brethren in the Eastern District of Pennsylvania 1708-1915*. Privately printed, 1915. BHLA Collection.

Personal manuscripts

Chalmer Faw, McPherson, Kansas
Gladys Mease, Goshen, Indiana
Jeff Glass, San Diego, California
James Benedict, Union Bridge, Maryland
Pearl Aldrich, North Liberty, Indiana
Jan Eller, Portland, Oregon
Christy Waltersdorff, Lombard, Illinois
Naomi Waggy, Goshen, Indiana
Craig Alan Myers, Columbia City, Indiana

Personal interviews

Graydon Snyder, Chicago, Illinois, January 13, 1998
Clarence Kulp, Harleysville, Pennsylvania, January 14, 1998
Ruth Fillmore, Buffalo Grove, Illinois, January __, 1998
Phyllis Carter, Goshen, Indiana, January 10, 1998